Above All Else

An Introduction to Life in Christ

CONCORDIA PUBLISHING HOUSE · SAINT LOUIS

7   8   9   10   11   12   13   14   17   16   15   14   13   12   11

Contents

Introduction

"You have exalted above all things Your name and Your Word" (Psalms 138:2).

What do you hold most precious? What are your life's highest priorities?

Above All Else introduces for you the basic truths of Christian doctrine. Each chapter presents the essentials of faith based on God's Word. The topics are not ancient stories with little relevance to life today. Instead, you will discover here the Good News of forgiveness, life, and salvation, Good News for the challenges, problems, and tragedies you experience every day.

Above All Else draws on Scripture and Luther's Small Catechism to present Law and Gospel to adult inquirers. This book is ideal for membership classes, a refresher course with fellow Christians, or personal study.

As you read and understand the Bible's key teachings for your life, may God—Father, Son, and Holy Spirit—strengthen you for living in Christ.

·1·
God Above All

The Christian faith centers on Jesus the Savior, who loved us and gave Himself for us. The Son of God became flesh and lived among us for a while, full of grace and truth. Christ is true God, we confess, and through Him we know God. Who is the God we worship?

GOD EXISTS

God is the source of everything. All things depend on Him. He has supreme authority, power, and wisdom. He is without beginning or end; He is always near us and yet fills the entire universe. He is holy and perfect in His being and in His dealings with His creatures. God is a being whose nature is goodness, power, and wisdom.

But how do we really know there is such a being? We cannot see, hear, or touch Him. Music is invisible, but we can hear it; air is invisible, but we can feel it; the sun can neither be heard nor touched, but we can see it and recognize its life-giving warmth. How then can we know God, who is beyond the reach of our senses?

Quite simply, we have a written record: the Bible. From its first to its last page, the Bible speaks of God as existing. He is not the creation of our own fancy. God is real, the greatest of all realities.

The Bible nowhere tries to prove the existence of God. But neither does it attempt to prove the occurrence of the great flood or the exodus from Egypt. Just as the Bible simply tells us about these events, so it simply tells us about God.

We May Know God

While we do not try to prove that God exists, we do find evidence of God's existence apart from the Bible. We often call this natural knowledge of God.

Most nations and races in history have believed in the existence of a supreme being. The fact that various peoples, even those living in isolation, have the same conviction of a supreme being is a strong argument for the existence of God.

Moreover, this world can hardly have originated by itself, nor can it have existed forever. If it were from eternity, there would be no change in it; for where there is change, there must be a beginning and an end. But the One who Himself is without beginning or end called the universe into being. This is known as the argument from the existence of the world.

Furthermore, we cannot fail to see beauty, order, and fitness in the world. Our hands are marvelously formed to do the work required of them. Our eyes, which give us the extraordinary ability of sight, are well protected by eyebrows and eyelids. Every part of our earth has plants and animals adapted to its climate. All of this testifies not only that a Creator exists but also that He is an all-wise being. The argument from design, then, testifies to the existence of God.

Finally, we are born with the conviction that there is a being who is above us and to whom we are responsible for everything we do. The voice of conscience inside every human being gives witness to the existence of a great Judge who will call us to account when our earthly lives are ended. We often try to silence our conscience and may for a while succeed in doing so. But eventually we submit to the insistent voice within us and acknowledge that there is a God.

The apostle Paul alludes to the natural knowledge of God in Romans 1:19–20. All people know of God's eternal power and majesty from the things He has made. Atheism, the view that there is no God, violates humanity's inmost convictions and runs counter to our observations. No person is an atheist by nature.

While this natural knowledge of God comes from Him and embraces many important truths, it cannot bring us salvation. When Adam and Eve fell into sin, they corrupted the perfect knowledge God had given them and reduced it to a shadow of what it once had been. As things are now, we by nature still know that there is a God. We know a number of His qualities. But we cannot say precisely who He is and what He is like. By nature we know that we are sinful, but we cannot find out how to rid ourselves of our guilt. We need more than this vague knowledge of God. So God has revealed Himself in specific ways.

God's Special Revelation of Himself

After Adam and Eve corrupted the knowledge of God in their hearts through sin, God mercifully spoke to them about Himself and His purpose. God has spoken to us. He did so not only in nature and in our conscience but also through a special revelation.

God has revealed Himself in the Scriptures. In the beginning God communicated directly with people. Later He called some into His service and gave them a message about Himself to convey to others. God led many of His prophets to put down in writing the message they had received. These are the books of the Old Testament.

At the right time the most astounding event of all came to pass: God sent His only Son to reveal to us the Father's heart of love and mercy. St. John describes this remarkable revelation: "No one has ever seen God. It is God the only Son, who is close to the Father's heart, who has made him known" (John 1:18 NRSV).

The Son of God, Jesus Christ, preached and taught and demonstrated His Father's love in His death and resurrection. He also sent special messengers, the apostles, to continue His gracious work. The Holy Spirit moved some of these messengers to record the Good News of Christ's saving mission and His ongoing work in His church. The New Testament contains the inspired writings of the Lord's apostles and evangelists.

God Himself addresses us in the Bible. He gave His Word in human language. This revelation shows the way to eternal salvation.

God Made the World

The world did not come into being by itself. Even our reason leads us to believe in an ultimate personal cause of everything that exists. The Bible speaks clearly and definitely about God the Creator: "In the beginning God created the heavens and the earth" (Genesis 1:1).

Of course, no human witnessed this event. We simply accept the Bible's inspired account by faith. Hebrews 11:3 affirms, "By faith we understand that the universe was formed at God's command, so that what is seen was not made out of what was visible." Creation, then, means that God made the world and all it contains out of nothing, employing only His Word.

Believers in evolution fall into two classes. Atheistic evolutionists deny the existence of a Creator, assuming that matter is eternal or that its origin is unknown. They hold that the world developed from some primary substance over a period of millions of years. Theistic evolutionists believe that God created the material from which the universe was formed and that everything developed from this basic material. For them evolution was God's method of creation.

Evolution is nothing more than a theory. Many of its points contradict specific statements of the Bible. For instance, the theory that higher forms of life developed from lower forms contradicts Genesis 1:11, 21, 24. God's people believe and confess that God created everything after its own kind. Rather than engage in speculations about the origin of the universe, we adore God for the grandeur and fitness of everything He created.

God Preserves and Governs the World

The Scriptures also tell us that the God who created the universe now preserves it. For example, He gives living creatures their daily food (Psalm 145:15); He guides the sun in its course (Matthew 5:45); and He provides us with all we require (Acts 14:17). What some people attribute to laws of nature (e.g., the sprouting of seed and the growth of plants), the Bible assigns to God's loving care and guidance (Psalm 104:14).

Christians believe that God watches over us every minute and keeps us from harm. When calamities and misfortunes come upon us, the Word of God assures us that He can bring good out of these experiences. God may use the hardships of life to turn us away from evil and to help us trust Him and seek His will.

Angels

The Scriptures tell us that God created not only the visible beings, which have material bodies, but also the invisible spirits, called angels. We do not know on which of the six days of creation the angels were made, but it is clear that their creation took place within that six-day period: "For in six days the Lord made the heavens and the earth, the sea, and all that is in them" (Exodus 20:11).

Some angels fell away from God (2 Peter 2:4); there are good angels and evil angels. The number of the good angels is very large (Daniel 7:10). They are powerful (Psalm 103:20); they will not and cannot fall away from God (Matthew 18:10; 1 Timothy 5:21); they engage in the praise of God (Revelation 5:11–14); and they are deployed by God to serve Christians (Hebrews 1:14). While we do not pray to angels or give them divine honor, we thank God for the help and protection He gives us through these messengers and servants. Scripture refers to special classes of angels: cherubim, seraphim, and archangels.

There also are many evil angels (Luke 8:30). The Bible frequently calls them devils. Their head is called Satan,

Beelzebub, or simply the devil. In mentioning their fall and everlasting punishment, Jude 6 implies that the evil angels were created holy. We do not know when they rebelled against God, but it must have preceded the fall of Adam and Eve. Satan, in the form of a serpent, was present in the Garden of Eden. Though Satan is strong and intent on harming and destroying Christians (1 Peter 5:8), we need not fear him. We are connected to the stronger one, Christ, who came to destroy the works of the devil (1 John 3:8).

Our Triune God

What God has told us in the Scriptures about His own being far surpasses our understanding. If God were a being like us, we could fully understand Him. But then He would not be God—the eternal, almighty, all-knowing Lord.

Christians confess the triune God, the one God in three persons. The Bible teaches that God is one divine being and that He is the only God. Yet God is three persons—the Father, the Son, and the Holy Spirit—and each person is equally divine and glorious. The mystery of the Christian faith is that we worship the Trinity, our Maker, Redeemer, and Sanctifier, who reveals Himself in His Word.

With thanksgiving for our salvation in Christ, we say: "Glory be to the Father and to the Son and to the Holy Spirit; as it was in the beginning, is now, and will be forever. Amen."

·2·

Humanity

Genesis 1 describes how God, after He made all other creatures, created the first people. God fashioned Adam by forming his body from the dust of the ground and by breathing into him the breath of life. God also made a wife for Adam out of Adam's own body. He created Adam and Eve in His own image, and He blessed them and appointed them to rule over all other earthly creatures.

The image of God includes qualities of the intellect, heart, and will. From Colossians 3:10 and Ephesians 4:24 we see that the divine image means having a knowledge, righteousness, and holiness similar to that of God. Adam and Eve were without sin, knew God, and were perfectly happy in Him. They were devoted to what is right and God pleasing and had a deep understanding of the divine will.

Evil Enters the World

Adam and Eve soon fell from the high position God had given them. They disobeyed a clear command of God (Genesis 3:1–6). Satan, taking the form of a serpent, suggested this sin. God did not force Adam and Eve to resist Satan's temptation, for He desired that they obey Him of their own free will. Yet Adam and Eve were not forced to give in to the devil. They chose to sin and were by no means unwilling victims.

That first act of disobedience brought disastrous consequences. Humans have kept some characteristics that distinguish them from animals—intellect and reason, the power of speech, conscience, and the soul. But in the fall humanity lost the most precious possession: the divine image. Sin also led to death (Genesis 2:17; Romans 5:12). Instead of loving God and continuing to be intimate with Him, Adam and Eve hid from their Maker in guilty fear. Now they knew by actual experience the difference between good and evil. It was a terrifying knowledge indeed!

Since Adam was the head of the human race, his guilt became the guilt of every person (Romans 5:12–21). Death, the punishment for sin, spread to all people. This does not mean that some individuals are innocent and merely treated as if they are guilty. Without exception, all have sinned and all equally deserve to die.

THE NATURE OF SIN

What is sin? Briefly, it is the violation of God's will as revealed in His Holy Law. Similarly, the Bible says, "Sin is lawlessness" (1 John 3:4). This simple statement emphasizes the seriousness of sin. Sin exists not only in mistakes that may be overlooked or in faults and shortcomings that may be excused. It exists in willful rebellion against the majesty of God. Every thought, desire, word, and action contrary to God's Law is sin. We must never trifle with sin; the Bible speaks of sin in tones of solemn warning (Exodus 20:5–6; Romans 3:9–20).

UNIVERSALITY OF SIN

The Bible teaches that all people are sinners. All people before the flood were tainted with wickedness (Genesis 6:5). Similarly, as the human race began again after the flood, God said about people: "every inclination of [their] heart is evil from childhood" (Genesis 8:21). History and each person's conscience attest to this fact. From the records of the past, we see that wrongs have been committed in every nation and society. Everyone can hear the accusing inner voice of conscience. While many differences exist among people, there is no difference in this: all have sinned and all are sinners.

Sinful at Birth (Original Sin)

The fall into sin brought about terrible results. Not only did Adam and Eve become sinful and mortal; they also passed this condition on to their descendants. *Original sin* refers not to something we do but to something we are by nature. It is inherited sin. A newborn baby is a sinful, impure being from the first moment of existence, because of original sin. We have inherited our sinful nature from Adam through our parents.

Some hold that infants sleeping peacefully in their mothers' arms are "innocent little angels." But the Bible teaches the reality of original sin in such passages as John 3:6 ("Flesh gives birth to flesh") and Ephesians 2:3 ("All of us also lived among them at one time, gratifying the cravings of our sinful nature"). Experience confirms this teaching of Scripture. We observe that wrong acts and attitudes are present among children even before they are able to learn these things from others. Because of original sin, humans by nature no longer have a perfect knowledge of right and wrong, and they desire to do evil.

Sinful in Life (Actual Sin)

Original sin is just as "actual," or real, as any other sin. However, we ordinarily use the term *actual sin* when we refer to those sins we actually commit. We sin not only in words and deeds but also in thoughts and desires. Jesus refers to our evil thoughts (Matthew 5:28; 15:19); we deceive ourselves if we deny our sinfulness. We may not have shocked our neighbors and associates by shameful or outrageous conduct, but we are guilty of sinning in our hearts and minds.

On the basis of the Holy Scriptures we speak of various classes of actual sins. Some of these groupings are sins of commission and omission (James 4:17); voluntary and involuntary sins (Romans 1:32; 1 Timothy 1:13); sins of weakness committed by Christians without deliberation, perhaps in rashness; and mortal sins that destroy faith.

These categories and definitions are valuable only as they serve to convince us that we are corrupt persons in desperate need of forgiveness. The sin of blasphemy against the Holy Spirit (Mark 3:28–29) is unforgivable because it involves persistent unbelief.

SIN RESULTS IN THE WRATH OF GOD

Why is sin such a terrible thing? First of all, it causes great distress in the world, as all people admit. The daily toll of crime and the heartache of war are the results of sin. Sin also causes suffering for the one who commits it. The wrongdoer must suffer consequences for the sinful action. But sin is most terrible because it is an offense against the Holy God. When Joseph was tempted to commit adultery, he replied, "How then could I do such a wicked thing and sin against God?" (Genesis 39:9).

Sin arouses the wrath of God, as Scripture and conscience both testify (Exodus 20:5; Ephesians 2:3). We may ask, is it not contrary to the nature of God, who is love, to be angry with His creatures? No, for God is also righteous and just (Romans 2:5–6). When His will has been violated, God's justice demands that the offender be held guilty in the court of heaven. The offender is then subject to the wrath of the Lawgiver and deserves His temporal and eternal punishment.

God punishes sin with all kinds of temporal afflictions. We see this from His curse upon humanity and the serpent in the Garden of Eden and from the flood. God also threatened Adam and Eve with death if they should disobey Him (Genesis 2:17). This included both physical and eternal death (separation from God's presence forever). Today all people are under the threat of eternal death, since all have disobeyed God.

Recognizing Our Sin

For a proper understanding of the Scriptures we first must answer the question, what is the Law? In the Law God reveals why He created us: to live to the praise and honor of our Maker and to serve our neighbors. The Law reveals what God demands of His creation; it tells us how we are to live. The Law also spells out the penalties for those who fail to live up to God's righteous expectations.

The Scriptures teach that God created Adam and Eve to be obedient creatures who would live according to His will and words. They knew God intimately. But after God gave an express command of Law (Genesis 2:16–17), they transgressed His command and their knowledge of God and His will became imperfect and indistinct. By nature Adam's descendants possess merely a blurred picture of the Law (good and evil) in their hearts. For fallen humanity, this partial knowledge is no longer a reliable guide (Romans 1:21; Ephesians 4:17–18).

Many centuries after creation God gave His Law in writing so that its content would be fixed and clear. God Himself wrote a part of it, the Ten Commandments (Exodus 20:1–17; Deuteronomy 5:1–21), on two tablets of stone (Exodus 34:28; Deuteronomy 5:22). God also elaborated and explained the Law to Moses and the other prophets, as well as to the apostles and evangelists, who have recorded it in the Bible.

Of course, not everything in the Bible is Law. God also revealed the Gospel, the Good News that in Christ there is hope for those who have broken the Law. Certain parts of the Law are no longer binding on Christians of the New Testament era. God intended some portions solely for the Israelites under the Old Covenant, as is shown by Colossians 2:16–17 and Galatians 4:10–11. Laws given to regulate the religious and political life of the Israelite nation are known as the ceremonial law and the political law.

The universality of sin becomes clear in the light of the Law. The Law demands more than abstaining from some evil deeds; it demands perfect holiness. Clearly, we cannot become children of God and enter eternal life through the Law, since this would require keeping the Law in its entirety (Galatians 3:10–12). Nevertheless, the Law is useful. It helps restrain wickedness on earth, making life bearable. In this respect it is like the bars of a cage that restrain wild beasts from causing destruction or like a curb that controls violent outbursts of sin and keeps order in the world. God's Law also serves as a guide to show His redeemed people His will for life in this world. Above all, though, the Law serves as a physician who makes a diagnosis and informs the patient of the serious nature of his illness. "Through the Law we become conscious of sin" (Romans 3:20). The Law cannot save us. It tells us that we cannot save ourselves and that we are lost if we rely on our own resources. But in this manner it prepares us to receive the news of God's forgiving and rescuing love in Jesus Christ, our Savior.

Life in Christ

God speaks to us in His Word through Law and Gospel. The Law teaches us what we are to do and not to do. The Gospel reveals what God has done, and still does, for our salvation. Through His Law God shows us our sin and threatens His wrath. Through His Good News He shows us His grace—love, mercy, forgiveness—in the Savior.

The church proclaims our faith in Christ, the world's Redeemer, the Lord who calls and strengthens us to follow in faith. He is our one foundation for life, our anchor for eternal life in heaven.

·3·

Jesus: Who He Is

As a result of the fall into sin, human beings are lost, sinful creatures, tainted with evil from the first moment of existence. By nature we are enemies of God and subject to divine wrath—unable to restore ourselves to the righteous state from which we have fallen. If God had abandoned the human race in this condition (for which we alone are responsible), no one could accuse Him of acting unjustly. But God did not intend to let people perish in the fire they foolishly had kindled. Before the world began, God decided on a work of rescue because He knew our desperate need. The rescue would violate neither His justice nor His mercy (Romans 3:24–26). The wrongdoing that had been committed had to be punished; justice demanded it. God's love, however, planned a way to save His fallen creatures.

God's Plan of Rescue

The Bible calls God's plan a mystery, because no person by nature knows of it. Poets and philosophers, who in certain respects show remarkable insight, display no knowledge of God's salvation (1 Corinthians 2:7–10). Only the Gospel reveals God's saving plan and purpose, and the Gospel focuses on Jesus Christ. The Gospel is the heart of the Bible, the greatest story ever told.

Rescue in the Fullness of Time

God's loving plan was to send a substitute for the human race. This person would fulfill our obligations, bear our sins, pay our penalties, and thus bring about our rescue. To accomplish such great things, our substitute had to have extraordinary qualifications. God's plan provided for our remarkable Savior.

Immediately after the fall, God let a ray of hope penetrate the gloom that had swiftly enveloped Adam and Eve. He promised a descendant who would crush the head of the serpent, though the Savior Himself would endure suffering (Genesis 3:15). As the centuries rolled by, God repeated His promise to send a deliverer, who would come from the people of Israel, from the tribe of Judah, and from the house of David. God revealed that this rescuer would be a great Prophet (Deuteronomy 18:15), a Priest (Psalm 110:4), and a King (Zechariah 9:9).

The climax of all of these prophecies came in Isaiah 53. Like an eyewitness to the event, Isaiah described how God's Servant would suffer and die as He took on Himself the load of human sin. As the Israelites spoke to one another of their Savior, they commonly referred to Him as the Messiah (Hebrew) or the Christ (Greek)—that is, the Anointed One (John 4:25).

The prophets pointed to a great moment in human history. Finally that moment arrived: the long-expected descendant was born. In Galatians 4:4 St. Paul speaks of this event as taking place "when the time had fully come," when the period of waiting was complete and God's appointed hour had arrived. The Savior born in Bethlehem was Jesus, the fulfillment of our hopes and the joy of Christian hearts.

CHRIST, THE GOD-MAN

Who is Jesus Christ? The Scriptures clearly reveal that He was a real man. He was born; He grew; He learned; He ate, drank, and slept. When He lacked food, He became hungry. He suffered pain. When He was nailed to the cross, He died. The Bible calls Him "the man Christ Jesus" (1 Timothy 2:5).

The same Scriptures also clearly reveal that Jesus is really God. He existed long before His birth, from eternity (John 1:1–3). He was conceived by the Holy Spirit (Matthew 1:20) and was born of a virgin. By His miracles He showed that He had divine power. After His death He rose again and ascended to heaven. The Scriptures call Him God (1 John 5:20) and the Son of God (Matthew 3:17). They assign the qualities of God to Him, such as omnipotence (Matthew 28:18) and omniscience (John 21:17). The Scriptures point out that Jesus is the creator and preserver of the universe (Colossians 1:16–17). He is given the same honor as the Father (John 5:23).

Christians confess what the Scriptures teach by saying that Christ has two natures: the divine and the human. The Bible never speaks of two Christs, always of one. Hence the two natures form one person and are not to be separated. The divine nature has existed from eternity, as we see from Psalm 2:7 ("today" refers to the day of God, which has no beginning or end). When Christ was conceived by the Holy Spirit, this divine nature added to itself the human nature (John 1:14). The two natures are inseparably united in what we call the personal union.

In this personal union each nature has its own particular qualities, which it shares with the other. Thus the divine nature possesses omnipotence, while the human nature, taken by itself, is not omnipotent. But, because of the personal union, the human nature shares in this great quality. We believe and confess "Jesus is almighty" and not "only His divine nature is almighty." Similarly, the human nature has the capacity to suffer and die, while the divine nature by itself does not. Through the personal union, however, the divine nature participates in this ability. "Jesus was crucified," we acknowledge. The one person, true God and true man, died on Calvary's cross.

The great acts Jesus performed for our benefit were not merely human acts, but human *and* divine acts. We have the assurance that His work is of tremendous value—the great cost required for our salvation.

Our Lord's Humiliation

Following the pattern of Scripture, we divide the life of Christ into two parts: the state of humiliation and the state of exaltation. The Bible says explicitly that Christ humbled Himself (Philippians 2:8). He could undergo this humiliation because He had taken into His person a real human nature. If He had nothing but the divine nature, this state would not have been possible for Him; for God is unchangeable (Malachi 3:6).

The humiliation of Christ is not the simple fact that He became a human being. It describes the manner in which He became a human being and the way in which He did His work. According to His human nature, Jesus did not always and fully use the divine qualities belonging to Him through the personal union. Because He is the God-man, He possesses omniscience; yet when He spoke to His disciples about the last things, He did not use this omniscience. Instead, humbling Himself, He said that He did not know the day and hour His Father had fixed for the world's judgment (Mark 13:32). But Jesus certainly possesses omnipotence. In Gethsemane He prayed, "Father, if You are willing, take this cup from Me" (Luke 22:42). He could at once have answered His prayer, but He refrained from using His almighty power and submitted to His Father's plan.

No one forced Christ's humiliation on Him. He took this state of His own accord for the redemption of the world (John 10:18). He became poor to make us rich (2 Corinthians 8:9). The various stages of the Savior's humiliation are His conception and birth; His life of poverty and lowliness; and His suffering, death, and burial.

The Savior in Exaltation

Christ did not remain in the state of lowliness and suffering. At His ascension, after His resurrection, He was exalted to divine glory and is now ruling in neverending majesty (Philippians 2:9–11; Ephesians 1:20–23). Christ is exalted according to His human nature. Just as the divine nature could not be lowered and humbled, so it could not be exalted. The exaltation of Christ means that, according to His human nature, He now unceasingly and fully uses His divine majesty to rule the universe and to bless and protect His church.

Christ's state of exaltation began as He came alive in the tomb and descended into hell. There He showed Himself to Satan and to the other condemned spirits as the victor (1 Peter 3:19). Afterward, He appeared to the women and His disciples on the first Easter morning. Forty days later came His ascension, when He bodily ascended into the glory of His Father to prepare a place for us in heaven. In His Word and Sacraments Jesus is still present with us to the end of the world (Matthew 28:20).

In connection with the ascension the Scriptures speak of Christ's sitting at the right hand of God (1 Peter 3:22). This is not one physical location, since God is not limited to a single place. Rather it signifies that according to His human nature Jesus now fully participates in governing the universe. Another great sign of Christ's exaltation will be His appearing to judge the living and the dead. At that time He will come in the clouds, and everyone will see Him and acknowledge Him as Lord.

Crown Him with Many Crowns

Crown Him with many crowns,
The Lamb upon His throne;
Hark how the heav'nly anthem drowns
All music but its own.
Awake, my soul, and sing
Of Him who died for thee,
And hail Him as thy matchless king
Through all eternity.

Crown Him the virgin's Son,
The God incarnate born,
Whose arm those crimson trophies won
Which now His brow adorn;
Fruit of the mystic rose,
Yet of that rose the stem,
The root whence mercy ever flows,
The babe of Bethlehem.

Crown Him the Lord of love.
Behold His hands and side,
Rich wounds, yet visible above,

In beauty glorified.
No angels in the sky
Can fully bear that sight,
But downward bend their burning eyes
At mysteries so bright.

Crown Him the Lord of life,
Who triumphed o'er the grave
And rose victorious in the strife
For those He came to save.
His glories now we sing,
Who died and rose on high,
Who died eternal life to bring
And lives that death may die.

Crown Him the Lord of years,
The potentate of time,
Creator of the rolling spheres,
Ineffably sublime.
All hail, Redeemer, hail!
For Thou hast died for me;
Thy praise and glory shall not fail
Throughout eternity.

Crown Him the Lord of heav'n,
Enthroned in worlds above,
Crown Him the king to whom is giv'n
The wondrous name of Love.
Crown Him with many crowns
As thrones before Him fall;
Crown Him, ye kings, with many crowns,
For He is king of all.

JESUS THE CHRIST

The name *Jesus* means "the Lord saves." The title *Christ* means "the Anointed." Christians boldly proclaims Jesus Christ as the Savior sent by His Father to bring us forgiveness and life. We trust that He alone has redeemed us from sin, death, and the power of the devil. We worship Him and receive His rich blessings through His Word and Sacraments. We serve Him, strengthened by the Holy Spirit to live in faith.

"Christ has died. Christ is risen. Christ is coming again. Alleluia."

·4·

Jesus: What He Has Done

The Father commissioned His Son to carry out the work of salvation, and Jesus Himself chose to do His Father's will. The Scriptures describe the mission that Christ fulfilled as Prophet, Priest, and King.

CHRIST AS PROPHET

Much of Christ's work on earth consisted of teaching: He was a true prophet. The task of God's prophets was not primarily to foretell future events; they did this only occasionally. God used prophets primarily to teach His people the grand truths He was revealing for our salvation. Prophets were not so much foretellers as *forth*-tellers of God's message.

Christ's career as a prophet began formally and publicly after His Baptism. Because of His ministry of preaching and teaching, the disciples and many other people regarded Jesus as a prophet (Luke 24:19). But there was a great difference between Christ and all others who came before Him. Even the greatest of God's prophets, such as Moses and John the Baptist, could proclaim divine truths only as these truths were supernaturally revealed. Jesus, however, possesses in Himself all wisdom and knowledge (Colossians 2:3). He could speak of God from personal acquaintance and with unique authority. He also confirmed that His teaching was divine by the many miracles He performed.

In part Jesus carried out His prophetic work directly, giving personal instruction to His disciples and to vast crowds. Many people who heard Him testified to the winsomeness of His words (Luke 4:22; John 7:46). In part

He carried out His work through His apostles and other messengers. This prophetic office of our Lord continues. While He no longer visibly moves among us to proclaim God's Word, He has made provision to carry on His mission. He calls all Christians to be witnesses to the great deeds of God and has established among us the office of the holy ministry. Whenever a Christian speaks the Word of God, he or she is a representative of Christ. The Lord also calls men into the public ministry of preaching and teaching His Word and administering His Sacraments. In this fashion the Savior carries out His prophetic office today, proclaiming Himself the Son of God and Redeemer of the world.

CHRIST AS PRIEST

Christ is also our Priest, our High Priest. This truth rests not only on the word of prophecy (Psalm 110:4) but also on some of the grandest and most comforting passages in the New Testament (Hebrews 7:25–28; 9:11–28).

What does it mean that Jesus is our Priest? Old Testament priests were the mediators between God and His people. By offering sacrifices they preserved or restored the right relationship between the Lord and the people of Israel. These priests brought offerings for the sins of the people in order to appease the Lord's anger. Of course, the validity and power of their sacrifices did not come from any inherent merit in the victims of the sacrifice. The great sin offering of the New Testament (the suffering and death of Jesus), which the Old Testament sacrifices prefigured, gave validity and power to those sacrifices.

Further, Jesus is the Mediator between God and the whole human race. God had given us His Law to keep. For a right relationship to exist between God and humanity, this Law had to be obeyed. But no mere mortal could measure up to the task, for God demands perfect obedience. It seemed that humanity, unable to meet this requirement, was doomed. Then Christ came as the rescuer of the race. To avert the disaster of eternal punishment for us, He had to take our place and keep the Law. This is exactly what He did as our High Priest. We find in His life a perfect obedience to all that God had commanded (Hebrews 5:8–20; Galatians 4:4–5; Matthew 3:15). Jesus did not perform this obedience for Himself; as God He is superior to the Law. He did all that He did for our benefit. We call this the active obedience of Christ. By fulfilling the Law in our place Jesus provides great comfort to us in life and death.

But far more was needed to secure our eternal welfare. Our many sins stood between God and us. Divine justice insisted that these sins be punished. The all-seeing eye of God beholds the wrongs we commit, both great and small, even those of which we ourselves are unaware. God can forgive, but He cannot simply overlook or ignore wrong-doing. Again and again the Bible tells us that God will repay each of us according to what we have done (Romans 2:6), which means that God will punish sin and will not lay aside His righteous judgment.

Either we ourselves have to pay the penalty for rebelling against God or someone else has to pay it for us. The penalty is death—eternal death—rejection from God's presence forever (Romans 6:23; Matthew 25:46). As our High Priest, Jesus came and bore this punishment for us. He became our substitute, as the Bible clearly testifies in 2 Corinthians 5:21 ("God made Him who had no sin to be sin for us") and Galatians 3:13 ("Christ redeemed us from the curse of the law by becoming a curse for us"). The guilt we had brought upon ourselves was counted as Christ's— as if He Himself had sinned. He is the sacrifice for our sins. His substitutionary death pays the price for our redemp-tion. In His passive obedience, Jesus suffered and died in our place.

Jesus Christ Is Risen Today

Jesus Christ is ris'n today, Alleluia!
Our triumphant holy day, Alleluia!
Who did once upon the cross, Alleluia!
Suffer to redeem our loss. Alleluia!

Hymns of praise then let us sing, Alleluia!
Unto Christ, our heav'nly king, Alleluia!
Who endured the cross and grave, Alleluia!
Sinners to redeem and save. Alleluia!

But the pains which He endured, Alleluia!
Our salvation have procured; Alleluia!
Now above the sky He's king, Alleluia!
Where the angels ever sing. Alleluia!

Sing we to our God above, Alleluia!
Praise eternal as His love; Alleluia!
Praise Him, all you heav'nly host, Alleluia!
Father, Son, and Holy Ghost. Alleluia!

How could divine justice punish an innocent person for the guilty? Christ voluntarily took the curse upon Himself, impelled by His great love for sinful humanity (Galatians 2:20). He freely accepted the guilt of humanity and the curse of sin and death.

Does the suffering of Jesus on the cross really remove our guilt and overcome sin and death? The Bible answers, Yes! Jesus' sacrifice was so powerful and effective because it was the sacrifice of a divine person, the Son of God (Hebrews 4:14; 7:26; 1 John 1:7). Since Jesus is both God and man, His blood has infinite power to cleanse, restore, and renew.

One of the most firmly established truths of the Bible is that Jesus, our High Priest, performed His work for all people: Christ is "the atoning sacrifice for our sins, and not only for ours but also for the sins of the whole world" (1 John 2:2). The entire punishment has been meted out;

the price has been paid in full.

Jesus is still active as our High Priest. Hebrews 7:25, Romans 8:34, and other passages depict Christ as our intercessor before the throne of divine majesty. He pleads for us, knowing our needs and weaknesses. We can be sure that God will not disregard the prayers of His own Son on our behalf. Our God will keep us firm in faith, anchored in His Word, to the Last Day.

CHRIST AS KING

The Bible also ascribes to Christ the function, or office, of King. In John 18:37 Jesus Himself claims this title. His kingdom is not a worldly one but a kingdom of grace. He lives and rules in the hearts of His followers, forgiving, renewing, and strengthening them by His love. Christ also governs the whole universe with almighty power and majesty (Ephesians 1:21–23). He is the head of the church, which He fosters, protects, and nourishes (Ephesians 5:23–27). When He returns in glory, He will lead His redeemed people home to heaven. He will also reign over His people in glory forever (2 Timothy 4:18).

SALVATION FOR ALL

In connection with the supreme importance of Christ's vicarious suffering and death, the Bible speaks of *atonement* (Romans 3:25; Hebrews 2:17). Atonement does not refer to something that takes place in us, but something that took place for us. It is an accomplished fact, not a continuous process. Atonement was made, once for all, when Jesus cried, "It is finished" (John 19:30). All human beings are beneficiaries of the atonement. It was prompted not by any human merit but solely by the grace and love of God in Christ.

Atonement (at-one-ment) means bringing enemies together in peace. Humanity had offended God. Christ reconciled the world back to God, taking its sins into

Himself and healing the breach (2 Corinthians 5:18–21). The Bible expresses the same truth through the term *propitiation* (KJV), or atoning sacrifice, which signifies that Christ appeased the anger of divine justice. Christ has removed the barrier of sin separating us from God and heaven. His atoning work

- frees us from the guilt of sin, because Jesus took upon Himself all the unworthiness and blame we incur by our wrongdoing;
- frees us from the penalty of sin, because Jesus bore the punishment we deserve (Isaiah 53:4–7);
- frees us from the dominion of sin, so that sin no longer has any claim on us as its slaves (1 Peter 1:18; Romans 8:1–11).

The church's faith rests on Jesus. He has redeemed us "from all sins, from death, and from the power of the devil." He took our guilt and punishment on Himself and set us free from slavery to sin. He triumphed over death. He completely conquered the devil.

The price? His "holy, precious blood" and His "innocent suffering and death." Thanks be to God who gives us the victory through our Lord Jesus Christ!

The Work of the Spirit

Imagine a prisoner condemned to die. While on death row, doctors discover that the man has cancer. To save his life, something will have to be done for him. His conviction must be successfully appealed in the courts or the governor must pardon him. But the man needs more. Something also must be done *in* him. The disease raging in his body must be checked or he will die in spite of his release.

This situation illustrates our position by nature. As transgressors of God's Law all people have been condemned to eternal punishment. Nothing except God's pardon can save us from this terrible fate. Jesus secured this pardon for everyone. As our High Priest He obtained for us God's complete forgiveness; heaven now is open to all people. But we need more than simply to hear about God's pardon. Something must be done for and in us too. Our faithless heart must be changed so that we receive the pardon Christ has won for us.

Our atonement, the work that had to be done for us, is complete. Christ carried out His work of redemption for the benefit of the whole world. God declares sinners—all sinners—righteous through the saving work of His Son. Our sins have been charged to Jesus; He takes to Himself the "sins of the world." God declares us not guilty because He is merciful and loving in Christ.

God also provides for our individual salvation. We receive forgiveness personally, through faith, as the Holy Spirit brings us to trust the Gospel.

Justification

A person who trusts in Jesus as Savior becomes spiritually alive and is justified by God. The whole human race was pardoned when Christ died on the cross, but faith in Christ receives God's pardon personally. St. Paul speaks of the marvelous act of God in Romans 3:21–22: "But now a righteousness from God, apart from law, has been made known, to which the Law and the prophets testify. This righteousness from God comes through faith in Jesus Christ to all who believe." The Law, the apostle shows, cannot make us righteous because we all have broken the Law. But God provided His righteousness for us apart from the Law. The Son of God demonstrated God's righteousness in His sacrificial death, and we receive it through faith in Jesus.

God justifies the guilty; He pronounces the sinner righteous. What induced God to declare us "not guilty"? Not any merit in us! It is the great work of Jesus Christ, who paid for our sins by His suffering and dying and rising to life. God justifies us by grace, for Christ's sake, through faith. Individuals receive the benefits of Christ's redemption.

Faith

Faith can have several meanings. Justifying faith is not a mere opinion or conjecture, but a conviction of the heart based on the sure promises of God (Romans 4:18–21). Faith is more than the belief that the Scriptures are true (although the believer gladly accepts the truthfulness of God's Word). Faith trusts in Jesus Christ as our personal Redeemer.

While faith involves a certain amount of knowledge, it is above all a matter of the heart. It requires simple trust rather than great learning. Moreover, the saving power of faith lies not in what it does but in what it receives and grasps: the blessings of Christ.

We also speak of the church's faith, or the Christian faith. Like the trust in our heart, *what* we believe is important. We confess the whole truth of God revealed in the Bible but summarized in the statement, "We are saved by grace, through faith in Christ, the Savior of the world."

REPENTANCE

Repentance, as ordinarily used in the Bible, consists of two "parts": recognition of our sinfulness and faith in Jesus Christ. First, we realize the damnable character of our sins and our helplessness to make atonement on our own. Second, in faith we seek refuge in the Savior. At times, however, the word *repent* is used in a restricted sense, referring simply to the recognition of our sinful condition.

REGENERATION

Regeneration refers to the work that God the Holy Spirit accomplishes in us. By nature we would reject the message that tells how Jesus has rescued us (1 Corinthians 1:23). The Scriptures call this condition a state of death (Ephesians 2:1). But God has graciously intervened and changed our attitude. He has given us believing hearts in place of unbelieving hearts. Christians have come from death to life by the power of God, through faith (Ephesians 2:4–9; Colossians 2:12–15). In mercy the Spirit works in our hearts so that we believe what we by nature despise. The moment we become believers in Jesus Christ, we become children of God. We are no longer spiritually blind and children of wrath. We have been born again, or regenerated (John 3:5). *Conversion*, a synonym of regeneration, signifies a sinner's turning to God through faith created by Him.

SANCTIFICATION

Faith is the beginning of a believer's new life. When we embrace Jesus as our Saviour, we begin a journey—a journey in Christ. We have passed from death to life and now walk the path toward our eternal home. Our whole lives have been changed. Though we once lived as enemies of Christ, we now live as His forgiven, renewed disciples. Though we once looked on God with anxiety, we now regard Him as our dear Father. We do not wish to offend our Lord but are eager to serve Him. "You have been set free from sin and have become slaves to righteousness," notes St. Paul (Romans 6:18). Christians have been redeemed and made spiritually alive so that we might serve God (Ephesians 2:10).

The Holy Spirit brings about this change of heart and life. The Spirit lit the flame of faith in our hearts through the Word and Sacraments. The triune God made His home in us (1 Corinthians 3:16; 6:19). The Bible asserts, "If anyone is in Christ, he is a new creation" (2 Corinthians 5:17). The old condition has actually passed away, and we have become new people. The Holy Spirit, who dwells in us, guides and empowers us. Through the strength He furnishes we avoid sin and gladly serve God and one another.

We are not perfect, however. As St. Paul rejoices in the new life, he also warns us against sin (Colossians 3:5). The apostle John urges us not to suppose that we are without sin (1 John 1:8). In Romans 7:14–25 St. Paul vividly portrays the struggle going on between the two natures of a believer: the "old Adam" that daily commits sin and the new nature that desires to serve God. The clash continues until the day of a Christian's death. Only in heaven will we be perfect (Hebrews 12:23).

We often use the term *sanctification* to describe the new life of the Christian. To sanctify is to make holy. Sanctification often describes the entire work of the Holy Spirit in God's children (calling, enlightening, and sanctifying), from the creation of faith to the moment of their death. In this sense, it includes conversion, the believer's life of service, and the continuing renewal of faith (1 Peter 1:2). The term is also used in a restricted sense, referring to a Christian's life of godliness (1 Thessalonians 4:3).

Good Works

Good works can be performed only by those who have been converted and who are a temple of the Holy Spirit (John 15:5; Romans 8:8).

By nature, dead in trespasses and sins, none of our attitudes or actions is acceptable to God. Of course, an unconverted person can perform deeds that we find highly commendable. Much noble service has been performed by non-Christian people. But the Scriptures insist that these deeds are not the fruit God desires. Since the Spirit of God is not dwelling in such people, they are sowing to the flesh and not the Spirit (Galatians 6:8). Their works do not come from the right motives, nor are they directed to the right end—the glory of God (1 Corinthians 10:31; Colossians 3:17).

However, every Christian performs good works. The indwelling Holy Spirit is active, continually leading Christians in the way of godly service (Romans 8:5). Every Christian remains imperfect. But the Spirit helps us in our weakness (Romans 8:26), and one battle after the other is won; one good work after the other is accomplished. While good works do not make us Christians, they are an indispensable sign that we are children of God. Without good works faith is dead.

What constitutes a good work in God's sight? It does not have to be something extraordinary and heroic, involving a dazzling exhibition of devotion to God. Extraordinary works are not in themselves the service that God desires. Good works in His sight are all thoughts, words, and actions that flow from faith, follow God's will, and thus bring glory to Him.

The Law of God shows Christians which works please God. From one point of view we do not need the Law. Because we are children of God and filled with the Holy Spirit, we spontaneously do what is right in God's sight. But Christians still have to contend with the sinful flesh that continues to cling to us. Therefore, we need this instruction to point out what is right and wrong. In Christ, we know that "love is the fulfillment of the law" (Romans 13:10).

PRAYER

As surely as all people live and breathe, God's people pray! The Christian is impelled by the Holy Spirit, who is a Spirit of prayer (see Romans 8:15, 26; Galatians 4:6). In prayer we speak to God in petition, intercession, and thanksgiving. We pray in the name of Jesus (John 16:23); we come to God in faith, trusting that He will hear our prayers because of the salvation Jesus has earned for us. Because of God's wise and loving providence, He does not always grant what we desire. In such cases He sees that another response will be better for us. Jesus teaches about prayer in Matthew 6:5–15 and Luke 11:1–13.

PREDESTINATION

God's work in us, as well as His work for us, is entirely the result of His mercy and love. The doctrine of predestination emphasizes this truth: God, who has graciously converted and sanctified us and our fellow Christians, in eternity thought of us and decided to save us, influenced by nothing but His grace. We find this teaching in Romans 8:28–30 and Ephesians 1:3–8.

Predestination gives all glory to God for our salvation. It also assures us that we need not be afraid as we face the future, because our Lord is providing for our eternal welfare. The church believes and lives in this Good News. When we realize the limitations of our knowledge as compared to the greatness of our God and the riches of His wisdom, we rejoice in the sure promises of His Word. We pray, "Come, Holy Spirit, fill the hearts of the faithful, and kindle in them the fire of your love. Alleluia."

·6·

The Bible

Inspired by God

What is unique about the Bible, this collection of sixty-six books written by prophets, apostles, and evangelists? The Bible itself tells us in 2 Timothy 3:16 that: "All Scripture is God-breathed". The Holy Scriptures that Timothy had known from his childhood—the writings of the Old Testament—are inspired by God and have come from God in every part.

Like the Old Testament, the New Testament writings are the Word of God. St. Paul says about his message: "This is what we speak, not in words taught us by human wisdom but in words taught by the Spirit, expressing spiritual truths in spiritual words" (1 Corinthians 2:13). Jesus Himself promised His apostles that "the Counselor, the Holy Spirit, whom the Father will send in My name, will teach you all things and will remind you of everything I have said to you" (John 14:26). The New Testament is God-breathed too.

The Bible is the inspired Word of God. The Bible comes from God. The words written by the prophets, evangelists, and apostles are God's own words. Since every word of the original text of the Bible is God's Word, we use the term *verbal inspiration*. God has spoken to us in every part of the Scriptures; His Word is completely reliable, true, and powerful.

What do the Scriptures themselves teach about their truthfulness? The prophetic and apostolic writings of the Old and New Testaments regard themselves as true and reliable in what they say and report. "All Your words are true," declares the psalmist (Psalm 119:160). Jesus and the apostles hold that Scripture must be fulfilled (Luke 22:37). The Old Testament was "written to teach us" (Romans 15:4; see also 1 Corinthians 10:11). What the Old Testament reports is unquestionably true. Jesus Himself says "the Scripture cannot be broken" (John 10:35).

THE UNITY OF SCRIPTURE

Jesus also says that the Scriptures "testify about Me" (John 5:39). He maintains that the words of Psalm 118:22—"the stone the builders rejected has become the capstone"—apply to Himself (Matthew 21:33–46). On the road to Emmaus, He teaches the disciples "what was said in all the Scriptures concerning Himself," beginning with Moses and the prophets (Luke 24:27). Speaking to His startled and frightened disciples following His resurrection, Jesus explains that "everything must be fulfilled that is written about Me in the Law of Moses, the Prophets and the Psalms" (Luke 24:44).

The apostles and the evangelists also teach that the Old Testament Scriptures witness to Christ. Peter identifies Jesus as the prophet about whom Moses wrote in Deuteronomy 18:15 (Acts 3:22). Philip explains Isaiah 53 to the Ethiopian eunuch as testifying to Jesus. The Acts of the Apostles concludes with the report that St. Paul spent the day from morning until evening testifying about the kingdom of God to the great numbers of Jews who came to his lodging. The apostle wanted "to convince them about Jesus from the Law of Moses and from the Prophets" (Acts 28:23).

Not only the Old Testament but also the apostolic writings of the New Testament find their center in Christ. The apostle John wrote so that people might believe that "Jesus is the Christ, the Son of God" (John 20:31). The apostle Paul writes to the Corinthians that he had decided not to come to them "with eloquence or superior wisdom," but rather that he had "resolved to know nothing while I was with you except Jesus Christ and Him crucified"

(1 Corinthians 2:1–2). In his Pentecost sermon, Peter says that God has made the Jesus whom they had crucified "both Lord and Christ" (Acts 2:36). From beginning to end, from Moses and the prophets to the Revelation of John, the Bible testifies to Jesus.

In its witness to Christ, Scripture is clear. Even children can understand its testimony; Paul reminds Timothy "from infancy you have known the Holy Scriptures" (2 Timothy 3:15). These writings are able to instruct us for salvation in Jesus Christ (2 Timothy 3:16). The Scriptures are, therefore, sufficient. They present a completely adequate revelation of God's will for the salvation of human beings and for their obedient response to His grace (2 Timothy 3:17). Finally, Holy Scripture possesses the power to produce an effect in those who hear or read it because God works through the words in the proclamation of His Law and His Gospel to work faith in human hearts. The Gospel is "the power of God for the salvation of everyone who believes" (Romans 1:16).

Reason and Faith

Since God has revealed Himself to us and has spoken to us in the Scriptures, we let the Scriptures be our guide.

One of the most dangerous opponents of the Word of God is human reason. Considered by itself, our reason is a grand gift from the Creator. Through reason we are able to learn, draw conclusions, evaluate, distinguish between right and wrong, and accomplish many other remarkable tasks. But through the fall into sin human reason was corrupted. People become proud and conceited, unwilling to bow before the authority of God or the Scriptures. The Bible says, "The sinful mind is hostile to God. It does not submit to God's law, nor can it do so" (Romans 8:7).

We Christians, too, regularly face the temptation to put our own reason above what God says. On the one hand, we could not learn and accept what God tells us in the Scriptures if we had no reason. On the other hand, however, we are in constant danger of rejecting God's teaching because our reason claims for itself the authority of deciding what is true and what is false in the revelation of God. The unwillingness of human reason to bow before the majesty of the Scriptures has led to many false teachings about Christ and His work of salvation. Scripture clearly warns that we must not be influenced by the negative, criticizing, unfavorable judgment of our reason when it urges us to disbelieve what God teaches in His Word.

Reason is an instrument, not the master, when we are studying the Holy Scriptures. Our reason helps us to see that the Bible teaches that God is triune. We must not use our reason, however, to sit in judgment on the question of whether or not this teaching is true. Like Mary, the mother of our Lord, we say, "May it be to me as You have said" (Luke 1:38).

THE WORD OF GOD

Along with Baptism and the Lord's Supper, the Word of God is a *means of grace*. These are the means by which the Holy Spirit offers us all the blessings of Christ and creates faith in us.

James 1:18 states, "He chose to give us birth through the word of truth." The apostle also writes, "Humbly accept the word planted in you, which can save you" (James 1:21). Christians are "born again, not of perishable seed, but of imperishable, through the living and enduring word of God" (1 Peter 1:23). The Holy Spirit works through the Word to create faith: "Faith comes from hearing the message, and the message is heard through the word of Christ" (Romans 10:17).

It is the Gospel, the message of Jesus and His saving work, that produces new life in us. St. Paul says in Romans 1:16, "I am not ashamed of the Gospel, because it is the power of God for the salvation of everyone who believes." In 1 Corinthians 1:17–18 Paul declares that the Gospel is foolishness to those who perish, but to those who are saved "it is the power of God." The Holy Spirit comes to us through the Gospel, a truth clearly proclaimed in Galatians 3:2. Here Paul asks, "Did you receive the Spirit by observing the law, or by believing what you heard?" The context clearly answers Paul's question. The Galatians received the Spirit by believing what they heard: they believed the Gospel.

God's Word informs and teaches. But it does—and must do—much more. Think of a man who is sinking into the mud of a deep swamp and appears to be doomed. A messenger arrives to inform him of a friend's willingness to come and help him. Is that enough to save him? No, he needs more than a message. He needs an actual rescue, a powerful arm pulling him out of what threatens to become a watery grave.

By nature we are bogged down in the quagmire of unbelief and slavery to sin. A mere announcement of our rescuer's willingness to come will not help us. Nothing short of the helper's actual appearance and His strong aid will suffice. The Word of God brings us this aid. It is indeed an announcement of God's grace, but it is more: it is the power of God converting the heart, planting trust in Jesus, and conveying strength to lead a Christian life.

Through the Gospel—revealed in the Word—the Holy Spirit kindles and preserves faith. God has chosen to work to save us and to keep us in fellowship with Himself through His Word and Sacraments. How, then, do we read Scripture for our spiritual nourishment and strength?

We recognize one literal meaning to the Bible. We read the words in their ordinary and natural sense, not reading our own ideas and prejudices into the Bible but hearing God speak in clear, understandable language.

We interpret the Bible in the context of the whole Bible. Passages that are difficult to understand may and should be interpreted in the light of other, clearer passages.

We read the Bible with a proper understanding of Law and Gospel. God confronts us in His Word with His holy demands and our many failures to obey His commandments. He also reveals His love and compassion in the Gospel, the saving truth that Christ has redeemed us with His blood and brought us forgiveness, life, and salvation.

Christians believe that sinners are declared right with God by grace alone, through faith alone, because of the merits of Jesus Christ alone. Our confidence is grounded in God's Word, the Holy Bible, and the Bible alone is the source and standard of our teaching and our life. As God's Word, the Bible is able to instruct us for salvation through faith in Jesus. In faith, we confess, "Your Word is a lamp to my feet and a light for my path" (Psalm 119:105).

·7·

Holy Baptism

How does the Holy Spirit accomplish the great work of converting and sanctifying us? God could by a mere act of His will impart His Holy Spirit and change our hearts. However, God chooses to use definite means in generating and nourishing the new life within us. These means of grace are the Word of God, Baptism, and the Lord's Supper.

The term *means of grace* does not occur in the Bible. Christians use the phrase to confess that God's grace operates through the Word and Sacraments to bring us salvation and forgiveness of sins. This term, then, signifies the channels used by God to bestow His grace. Electricity exists in abundance all around us, but to receive its benefits in our homes, offices, and workplaces we use the channels: transformers, cables, and wires. Similarly, God's rescuing power and grace surround us on all sides, but we receive His gifts through the instruments He has designated.

The means of grace are not mechanical or magical. We do not perform certain acts and immediately receive the benefits. The posture of the heart does matter. Receiving the benefits of the means of grace requires genuine faith in Jesus. God's grace is resistible; we can reject His salvation in Christ. The means of grace never operate automatically. Yet God has promised to work through the Word and Sacraments, and the Holy Spirit is always present, drawing sinners to Christ, whenever and wherever we find the means of grace.

The word *Sacrament* also does not occur in the Bible. A Sacrament is a sacred act, instituted by God Himself, involving the use of certain visible elements and conferring the forgiveness of sins. These characteristics are found in Baptism and the Lord's Supper.

The Sacraments are not separate from the Word of God. All of the means of grace have a common element, the Gospel, that gives each its power. The Bible is the written Word of God, and the Sacraments are the visible Word of God.

WATER AND THE WORD

Our Lord Jesus instituted Baptism. Before He ascended to heaven, Christ gave His disciples the Great Commission: "Go and make disciples of all nations, baptizing them in the name of the Father and of the Son and of the Holy Spirit" (Matthew 28:19). On the first Christian Pentecost, Peter said to the multitude in Jerusalem: "Repent and be baptized, every one of you, in the name of Jesus Christ for the forgiveness of your sins" (Acts 2:38). Ananias, a devout disciple of Jesus, said to the sightless Paul: "Get up, be baptized and wash your sins away" (Acts 22:16). The early church regularly baptized all kinds of people, for God's people confessed that in Baptism God forgives us and incorporates repentant sinners into His church, His redeemed people in Christ.

THE NATURE OF BAPTISM

Baptism is the application of water to individuals in the name of the triune God at the command and promise of God. The visible means used in Baptism is water, applied "in the name of the Father and of the Son and of the Holy Spirit." The water of Baptism is not just plain water; it is "water included in God's command and combined with God's Word."

Not all Christians agree on the manner of applying the water. Some hold that Scripture requires bodily immersion. Some prefer sprinkling water on the forehead. The word *baptize* in the New Testament covers a variety of washings. Baptisms were performed in various places and with different amounts of water. Jesus "went up out of the water" after His Baptism (Matthew 3:16). Philip and the Ethiopian official went "into the water" (Acts 8:38). The 3,000 people who joined the Christian church on Pentecost were baptized, perhaps in different parts of the city (Acts 2:41). In summary, then, the Bible does not teach that God has ordained a specific method of applying the water in Baptism. While Baptism may be performed by immersion, God does not say it must be performed in this manner.

BENEFITS OF BAPTISM

The benefits of Baptism are among the most comforting promises in the Bible. Baptism makes us children of the triune God, recipients of His blessings. In Baptism, God works forgiveness of sins, rescues from death and the devil, and gives eternal salvation to all who believe.

The Lord Jesus instituted Baptism to serve until His return as an instrument or a means to offer and convey the benefits of His death and resurrection. It is not, therefore, primarily a sacred rite symbolizing the sinner's need for spiritual cleansing. Nor is its chief purpose to offer the individual an opportunity to make a public profession of faith in obedience to one of God's ordinances. Holy Baptism is a means of grace. It is not a channel through which the sinner approaches God, but a channel through which God approaches the sinner in grace. Through water as an external means, God Himself offers and bestows the forgiveness of sins, life, and salvation. Baptism shows God in action, working through water and His Word, reaching out in grace to the lost.

The Sacrament of Baptism has been called the "visible Word," since it imparts to repentant sinners the same benefits and blessings offered and conveyed in the Gospel. What are Baptism's blessings?

- Forgiveness of sins (Acts 2:38). Baptism washes away sin (Acts 22:16). It sanctifies and cleanses the church so that it is "radiant … without stain or wrinkle or any other blemish, but holy and blameless" (Ephesians 5:27). Baptism regenerates and gives the repentant sinner a good conscience toward God (1 Peter 3:21).

- Baptism bestows the gift of the Holy Spirit. On Pentecost Peter proclaimed, "Repent and be baptized, every one of you, in the name of Jesus Christ for the forgiveness of your sins. And you will receive the gift of the Holy Spirit" (Acts 2:38). The Spirit, given in Baptism, dwells within us and makes us spiritually alive, assuring us that we are the children of God and co-heirs with Christ. The Spirit intercedes for God's people, causing us to live according to God's will and preserving us in the true faith (Romans 8:8–11, 14–17, 38–39).

- By Baptism the child of God is brought into a mystical union with Christ, dying with Him on the cross, being buried with Him, and rising with Him to a new spiritual life. As a result, the baptized are in a new relationship with Christ. We have a new identity; we are a new creation, sons and daughters of God, no longer slaves of sin but slaves to righteousness (Romans 6:3–13; 1 Corinthians 6:9–11).

- Through repentance and Baptism the Holy Spirit incorporates all believers into the Christian church. As members of the body of Christ, we enjoy all the blessings of the people of God. We are enabled by the Holy Spirit to serve our Lord and one another with the gifts and talents that God has given us (1 Corinthians 12:14–27; Romans 12:4–8).

- Baptism serves the unity of the church and the Christian home. The apostle Paul sees Baptism as one of the most important reasons for the people of God to make every effort to maintain in their midst the unity of the Spirit in the bond of peace (Ephesians 4:3–6). He urges his fellow Christians to remember that they were baptized in the name of Christ, not in the name of Paul or Apollos or Cephas (1 Corinthians 1:10–13). Christ is the head of the church, and in Him there is unity. By Baptism, we are made members of the body of Christ, regardless of nationality, culture, gender, and social status (1 Corinthians 12:13; Galatians 3:27–28).

- The apostle Paul also relates Baptism to Christian love and unity in the home. He exhorts husbands to love their wives as "Christ loved the church and gave Himself up for her, to make her holy, cleansing her by the washing with water through the word" (Ephesians 5:25–26).

- Baptism dispels all the fears that Christians face in their life as a result of sin, death, and the power of the devil.

The Holy Spirit, forgiveness of sins, life, and salvation—these are the gifts we receive in Holy Baptism. They are certainly bestowed where they are received in faith. Human reason cannot understand how water and words can be the source of such great blessings. But God, not our reason, decides the significance of His Sacraments.

The benefits of Baptism last throughout life. The Sacrament does not have to be repeated when a person who has fallen away from God returns to Him in true repentance. In Baptism God gives us the gracious promise that we shall be His own; this promise will never lapse (Romans 3:3–4; 2 Timothy 2:13). Sometimes we are burdened by a sense of our sinfulness and look for God's assurance that our sins are forgiven. At such times our Baptism is a solid rock on which to stand. Here we can find the solace for which our heart is yearning.

Unbelief, not the lack of Baptism, leads to condemnation (Mark 16:16). Hence, if a believer who has not been baptized dies, he or she will be saved.

Baptism Is for All People

The Bible teaches Baptism is for everyone, infants as well as adults. In instituting this Sacrament Christ says that all nations are to be baptized (Matthew 28:19); this includes children. Moreover, Jesus nowhere excludes children from this Sacrament. In fact He insists on Baptism as the means to welcome God's children into His family (John 3:5). He definitely states that in His kingdom there are children (Mark 10:14). The New Testament declares Baptism to be the counterpart of circumcision, which was performed on infants seven days old (Colossians 2:11–12). The Bible also states that the apostles baptized entire households; children certainly were included (Acts 16:15, 33; 1 Corinthians 1:16).

Jesus Himself indicates that children can have faith when He refers to the "little ones who believe in Me" (Matthew 18:6). The Spirit creates faith even in infants who are unaware of what is happening to them and unable to understand the meaning of Baptism. (See the case of Elizabeth's unborn child, Luke 1:15, 44.) Sponsors who witness the Baptism can later remind their god-children of this washing and renewal in the Holy Spirit.

Adults usually receive instruction before they are baptized. This was the practice of the apostles, as in the case of the Ethiopian official (Acts 8:35–38). Since adults agree to be baptized, the church does not generally require sponsors.

LIVING IN OUR BAPTISM

Baptized into Christ's death and resurrection, we live in faith toward God and in fellowship with His church. Our sinful nature, the Old Adam, is drowned every day as we remember our Savior's gifts of forgiveness, life, and salvation for us. The new nature, connected to Christ and strengthened by the Spirit, seeks to serve God and to live to His praise and glory.

We remember our Baptism by speaking the words, "In the name of the Father and of the Son and of the Holy Spirit." We call to mind our Baptism when we make the sign of the cross—the mark of Christ the crucified. We confess before the world our baptismal faith and identity as we worship our triune God. "I am baptized!"

We are the church; we are baptized into Christ!

·8·

The Lord's Supper

Like the Word of God and Baptism, the Lord's Supper (or the Sacrament of the Altar) is a means of grace through which the Holy Spirit offers us all the blessings of Christ and creates faith in us. Like Baptism, the Lord's Supper is a Sacrament. It is a sacred act, instituted by God Himself, involving the use of external elements and conferring the forgiveness of sins. The Gospel provides the Lord's Supper with its forgiving, renewing, and strengthening power.

On the night He was betrayed, Jesus gathered His disciples to celebrate the Passover. This meal commemorated God's rescue of His people from slavery in Egypt. A lamb without blemish, unleavened bread, and wine were shared as families told the story of their salvation.

Jesus' Last Supper with His disciples on the first Maundy Thursday was more than a Passover meal. The Lord instituted His own memorial meal, a meal to be observed until He returns in glory. His Supper consists of bread and wine, and in, with, and under the bread and wine the Lord gives His body and blood.

The New Testament contains four accounts of the institution of the Lord's Supper (Matthew 26:26–28; Mark 14:22–24; Luke 22:19–20; 1 Corinthians 11:23–25). The Lord's evangelists and apostles recognized something important and holy in this meal.

REAL PRESENCE

In the words of institution Christ says, "This is My body. ... This is My blood." Some believe that the sacramental bread and wine cease to be earthly elements and *become* the body and blood of Christ. (This is known as the doctrine of transubstantiation.) But the Bible nowhere speaks of such a change of substance. St. Paul expressly calls the sacred elements as they are used in Holy Communion "the bread" and "the cup" (1 Corinthians 11:26–28). Furthermore, the apostle implies that the sacramental bread and wine remain bread and wine, though they are united with Christ's body and blood (1 Corinthians 10:16).

Some assert that the real presence of Christ in the Sacrament is too great a mystery, too incredible a miracle. They deny that communicants—those who eat and drink the bread and wine—receive the body and blood of the Savior. At most they are willing to admit that a symbolic eating and drinking of Christ's body and blood take place. Others insist that Christ's body is in heaven, far removed from earth. Therefore, they say, it is impossible for Jesus to give His body and blood in the Sacrament. Still others hold that the sentence "This is My body" is a figure of speech; the word *is*, they assert, means "signifies." They claim that since we do not see or taste Christ's body and blood, these elements cannot be in the Sacrament. They also argue that Jesus' body and blood cannot be at many different places at the same time, as is necessary for services at the same time around the world.

Because the Lord's Supper is a divine institution, we trust the Word of Christ.

In the Lord's Supper there is present the true body and the true blood of Jesus Christ. This real presence reflects the consistent witness of Scripture: the Supper is what our Lord has said it is. The realistic language in Scripture, both in the foretastes of the Supper in the Old Testament as well as in the actual supper on the night when Jesus was betrayed, invites us to believe God's Word. There is no ambiguity in Christ's words. The body and the blood of our Lord are, as He said, present.

This real presence takes place in, with, and under the blessed bread and wine. The body and blood of Christ are really present and are eaten and drunk orally by the communicants in the meal. But bread and wine also are eaten and drunk orally. This happens, mysteriously, by the almighty power of Christ Himself through His Word.

The body and blood of Christ should be taken by eating and by drinking. Because of the sacramental union, the true body and blood of Christ are orally received in the Lord's Supper by all who eat and drink the consecrated bread and wine. The bread and wine are eaten and drunk with the mouth, in a natural way, just as one eats any other food or drink. The body and blood of Christ one also eats and drinks with the mouth, but in a supernatural or incomprehensible way.

This eating and drinking with the mouth is done by all communicants, even those who are unworthy, impious, or unbelieving. The unworthy communicant (that is, one who does not have faith in Christ's words) receives sacramentally the body and blood of Christ under the bread and wine, but he or she does not receive spiritually the blessing of the Sacrament. On the contrary, the unworthy communicant receives judgment and potential condemnation from such eating and drinking.

The Sacrament consists of the entire action of Christ in His institution. He blessed or consecrated the bread and cup; He distributed the earthly elements. He also spoke the words, "This is My body. … This is My blood." This is what Jesus did at the first meal, and this is what the disciples were commanded to do in remembrance of Christ.

Blessings of the Lord's Supper

The Lord's Supper is "visible" Gospel; it conveys the same glorious treasures as the spoken and written promises of God in Christ. When our Savior instituted the Lord's Supper, He stated that He was imparting to His disciples the very body that was to be given for them on the cross and the very blood that was to be poured out for them. This was the "ransom money" to be paid for our release from sin and death. The Lord acted as a friend who has paid a debt for us and shows us the canceled check to assure us that the payment has been made.

Jesus also calls the cup "the new covenant in My blood" (Luke 22:20). In this Sacrament He establishes a new covenant with us, a covenant different from that of the Law. The new covenant, or testament, rests on divine love and grace, conveying to us the forgiveness of sins. When we approach the Lord's Table in true faith, we certainly receive the pardon that God gives there freely and abundantly.

The benefits to be received by faith through the eating of this holy meal are many. In the broadest sense, they consist in all the fruits of Christ's atoning work, which are offered, given, and sealed to communicants through this means of grace.

- Forgiveness of sins. The Lord's Supper was given, and is received, for the forgiveness of sin (Matthew 26:28). Through this meal, as Jesus says, sins are forgiven and Christians are restored again to wholeness in God's sight.

- Strengthening of personal faith. God's promise of grace and life is never uncertain in itself. But when faith wavers, the promise seems uncertain. Our faith is never so strong that it has no need of strengthening: "So, if you think you are standing firm, be careful that you don't fall!" (1 Corinthians 10:12). It is most comforting to know that faith in the forgiveness of sins is preserved and strengthened through the Sacrament. The Lord's Supper does not produce uncertainty. It offers assurance and comfort as Christians eat the body and drink the blood of our Lord and so "proclaim the Lord's death until He comes" (1 Corinthians 11:26).

- The unity of the church. Through this eating and drinking a bond of unity between God's people is nurtured and strengthened. Communicants are united with one another in the body of Christ. This is St. Paul's point in 1 Corinthians 10:17: "Because there is one loaf, we, who are many, are one body, for we all partake of the one loaf."

- The "mystical union" between the believer and Christ. According to St. Paul, through the eating of this blessed bread and wine we are united with Christ: "The cup of blessing which we bless, is it not the communion of the blood of Christ? The bread which we break, is it not the communion of the body of Christ?" (1 Corinthians 10:16 NKJV). The union of faith, the mystical union, between the individual recipient and Christ is nurtured when the Lord's body and blood are taken into the mouths of those whom He has chosen to be His own. (In Baptism, too, Christ has taken us into His saving death and resurrection.)

- Everlasting life. The Lord's Supper bestows upon those who receive it everlasting life. Believers already have life and salvation, completely and in its fullness. Yet because the Lord says that life and salvation are to be received through this meal, Christians desire to receive what is already theirs.

Who Should Commune?

St. Paul says that we should examine ourselves before we partake of the Lord's Supper (1 Corinthians 11:28). Therefore we do not administer this Sacrament to children who are unable to examine themselves or to people who for any reason do not and cannot confess their sins and desire forgiveness.

The Gospel blessings of the Lord's Supper are more than enough to move one to receive the Sacrament as often as possible. Beyond that, however, another motivation for the frequent reception of the Supper is to be found in the command and invitation of Christ. This Supper is not optional for us. Jesus uses imperative verbs: "take," "eat," "drink," and "do." Christ wants these things to be done and in no way neglected or despised. Even if there were no benefit attached to the Lord's Supper, the fact that our Lord invites and commands us to partake of it would still move us to receive it—and to receive it often. We hear these commands as gracious invitations to receive what Christ offers.

All who commune in our church should confess their faith pertaining to the real presence of Christ in the Holy Supper. *Close Communion* is the practice of admitting only persons of the same confession to our altars. The intimacy involved in communing together presupposes oneness of faith, attesting that those who commune together agree with one another (1 Corinthians 10:17). Therefore we cannot admit to our table those who have a different confession about Christ and His Supper. A person who has committed a faith-destroying sin and has apparently not repented must also be excluded from the Sacrament. The Bible says that such a person "eats and drinks judgment on himself" (1 Corinthians 11:29).

The church confesses in the Lord's Supper the Good News of Christ crucified and risen for our forgiveness, life, and salvation. What priceless treasures are ours through eating and drinking, in faith, His body broken and blood shed for us. We give thanks to our Lord, who refreshes us with His gifts and strengthens us to live in faith and love.

·9·

The Church

The English word *church* comes from a Greek word meaning "the Lord's" or "belonging to the Lord." Originally the term designated the house of worship of Christians living in Greek-speaking countries. When the Bible was translated into English, *church* was used to translate another Greek word that basically means "an assembly or meeting." The Latin form of this word is *ecclesia*. The word signifies a building used for divine worship. Its other meanings, such as a local congregation or a larger religious body, are derived meanings.

The Church Universal

In response to Peter's confession of faith, Jesus said, "On this rock I will build My church, and the gates of Hades will not overcome it" (Matthew 16:18). Christ promised that He will establish His church on earth, and He fulfilled His promise. In Ephesians 1:22–23 St. Paul states that God "placed all things under His [Christ's] feet and appointed Him to be head over everything for the church, which is His body." In Ephesians 5:25–26 the apostle affirms that Christ "loved the church and gave Himself up for her to make her holy, cleansing her by the washing with water through the word."

The picture of the church as the body of Christ becomes especially clear in 1 Corinthians 12:12–13: "The body is a unit, though it is made up of many parts; and though all its parts are many, they form one body. So it is with Christ. For we were all baptized by one Spirit into one body—whether Jews or Greeks, slave or free—and we were all given the one Spirit to drink."

Church and *body* are collective terms, referring to a large number of individuals. The Holy Spirit, who works through the means of grace, makes these people members of the "universal" church. The church, therefore, is the body of Christ, the communion of saints, the total number of those who believe in Christ as their Savior.

The church is God's people, united by faith in Jesus and the gift of the Holy Spirit. The church is found where the Gospel is preached in its purity and the Sacraments are administered according to the Gospel.

The church is universal. It is not confined to a certain locality or human organization but is found wherever there are children of God in Christ. We sometimes call the church *catholic*, a synonym of universal. Since the church is universal, believers who hold membership in other denominations are also members of the body of Christ.

Every believer in Jesus is a member of the church. No non-believers are members. Since only believers receive eternal life, it follows that one must be a member of the universal church to enter heaven. Therefore we say there is no salvation outside the church—no salvation apart from the body of Christ.

The universal church also has other characteristics. Because it is the body of Christ, the one body, the church possesses unity (Galatians 3:28). The church is also holy, having been cleansed by Christ Himself, who redeemed us and called us into His fellowship (Ephesians 5:25–27). This perfect holiness consists in the holiness of the Son of God, our Savior, which has been credited to us. In addition, all members of the church serve the Lord in holiness of life, though this holiness remains imperfect on account of our inborn sin.

Christian and apostolic, based on the apostles' proclamation of the Gospel and sent into the whole world, the church is also indestructible, as Jesus Himself declared (Matthew 16:18). Particular denominations come and go, but the church of Jesus Christ will endure until the end of time.

Since the church is built by the Holy Spirit working through the means of grace, we call the means of grace the marks of the church. Where the Gospel, Baptism, and the Lord's Supper are in use, we may expect to find members of the church.

The Church: Invisible and Visible

We also refer to the universal church as the *invisible church*. Only God can know who all the members are. We use the term *visible church* to refer to all people on earth who profess to be disciples of Jesus Christ and believe in the triune God. When we speak of the whole Christian church on earth, we usually think about various denominations and church organizations. Their membership often includes true Christians and those who bear the Lord's name falsely. God's people seek a church body and congregation that teach the Word of God in its truth and purity and administer the Sacraments as Christ commanded.

The Local Congregation

The word *church* does not always refer to the sum total of believers. St. Paul writes to the churches of Galatia (Galatians 1:2). St. John writes to the seven churches in Asia (Revelation 1:4). The word *churches* signifies local congregations.

God desires that Christians who live in a particular area gather together in a local church or congregation. Churches arose wherever the apostles preached. In Matthew 18:15–17 Jesus acknowledges that His disciples, wherever they are, will form churches whose members can admonish an erring brother or sister. Hebrews 10:25 warns Christians not to forsake their assemblies or meetings. God intends His children to have contact with one another and to use the means of grace together.

The church exists because of God's intention and plan to gather to Himself a people set apart and dedicated to Him. The church was created and is built and preserved by the grace and power of the triune God. The triune God dwells among, is in close association with, and is actually in a spiritual union with His people, the redeemed of the Lord (2 Corinthians 6:16–18; Ephesians 2:20–22; 1 Peter 2:5). The same God and Father who raised Jesus Christ from the dead is, by His almighty power, also raising sinners from spiritual death to lives of faith with Christ.

The members of Christ's church are a flock of lambs or sheep (Luke 12:32; John 10:1–21, 27; Acts 20:28), children of God (John 1:12; Romans 8:16–17, 21), "those called" (1 Corinthians 1:24; Romans 8:28), "saints" (2 Corinthians 1:1; Ephesians 1:1), "members of God's household" (Ephesians 2:19), "a holy priesthood" (1 Peter 2:5), and "a royal priesthood, a holy nation" (1 Peter 2:9). In the Book of Acts members of the church are usually called "disciples."

These and similar words portray the church as the people of God, who are related to Jesus Christ by faith, who hear His Word, and who desire to serve Him. The church consists of many different types of individuals, but we are not individuals in isolation. We are a fellowship of believers. In bringing people to Baptism and faith in Christ, the Holy Spirit first unites us to Christ and then, through Him, to one another. This living, spiritual organism has the characteristics, endowments, and functions of a human body. United with Christ, our head, we are endowed with the gifts of salvation: faith, forgiveness of sins, spiritual life, the hope of heavenly inheritance, the power to overcome sin, and the ability to serve others in the body of Christ as well as in the world at large, as the Spirit wills.

God in His grace planned from eternity to use the church as an instrument through which He would make known His saving purpose to all the world. Christ gave His disciples the Great Commission, the mission of the entire church to the very end of the age (Matthew 28:19–20). To carry out their divine mission, Christ has entrusted to the church the Office of the Keys: the authority to preach the Gospel, administer the Sacraments, remit and retain sins.

This authority was given to the entire church and not only to certain individuals. The local church has this authority and power as priests and kings before God. As children of God by faith in Christ, they are also members of the body of Christ to whom Paul says: "All things are yours" (1 Corinthians 3:21, 23; 12:27).

With the Office of the Keys, members of a local church have been given the authority and the responsibility to make provisions for the faithful use of the Word both in the home and in the congregation. They also are expected to watch over both the doctrine taught and professed in their midst and their own conduct, so that as they are led and sustained by the Spirit, they may together be a credit to the Gospel and to their profession of faith.

In addition, a Christian congregation is to encourage and exhort its members to serve one another with the spiritual gifts and talents that God has given to each for the common good. In this way, by speaking the Word of God, the body of Christ may be built up in faith, hope, and love. This also includes acts of love on behalf of the sick, lonely, discouraged, and all who are in need of help both within and outside the congregation. We will use our spiritual gifts and perform our various tasks in the church in a spirit of peace and unity.

A Christian congregation exists to make disciples, to carry out the Great Commission in its community and through association with other Christian congregations, to the outermost parts of the earth. By bearing witness to the Gospel of Jesus Christ, it calls people to repentance and to faith. It seeks to equip its members to speak the truth with love, to live lives that would commend the faith to others, and to account with gentleness and reverence for the hope that is in us.

CHRISTIAN FELLOWSHIP IN THE CHURCH

Unity in Christ is a gift that the Holy Spirit bestows on the people of God when He brings us to faith. He thereby unites us in a mystical union with the Savior and also places us in a spiritual relationship with all other Christians. Through faith we become children of one heavenly Father, members of the family of God, and joint heirs of eternal life.

This is a spiritual unity, but it is not a static relationship. It is a unity through which the Spirit creates within the people of God the desire to work toward external unity and fellowship with all who confess faith in Christ. This unity is rooted and grounded in the triune God's eternal purposes for His church. It is God's will that this Spirit-given unity may become manifest as Christians through the Word "reach unity in the faith and in the knowledge of the Son of God and become mature, attaining to the whole measure of the fullness of Christ" (Ephesians 4:13).

God desires that the doctrine taught in the church be in agreement with His Word, so that the church may not be "tossed back and forth by the waves, and blown here and there by every wind of teaching" (Ephesians 4:14). Instead, speaking the truth in love, Christians "will in all things grow up into Him who is the Head, that is, Christ" (Ephesians 4:15). Moved by Christian love, we look for ways to build up our fellow believers in faith. God desires that Christians make every effort to keep the unity of the Spirit in the bond of peace.

Divisions are the result of sin. They dishonor Christ and often indicate human immaturity and pride. Divisions also result when false teachers arise within the church and distort the truth in order to gain their own following (Acts 20:29–30). The Bible therefore exhorts the church to profess the truth courageously. At the same time we are to guard the flock of Christ against the intrusion of false teachers.

The church lives in Christ together. Baptized into His death and resurrection, we serve our Lord and one another in the grace and power of the Holy Spirit. We are Christ's holy people, His disciples in mission to the world.

The Ministry

Every Christian is a member of the body of Christ. Every believer is also a priest of the Lord. When St. Peter addresses God's people as "a royal priesthood" (1 Peter 2:9), he refers not simply to apostles, pastors, and teachers but to all Christians. Through Baptism, all God's people, without exception, are priests; we serve in His holy temple, the Christian church.

After Peter made his great confession that Jesus is the Messiah, Jesus said to him: "I will give you the keys of the kingdom of heaven; whatever you bind on earth will be bound in heaven, and whatever you loose on earth will be loosed in heaven" (Matthew 16:19). Jesus did not give special status to Peter, for He later spoke the same words to all the disciples (Matthew 18:18). The risen Lord breathed on His disciples and said: "Receive the Holy Spirit. If you forgive anyone his sins, they are forgiven; if you do not forgive them, they are not forgiven" (John 20:22–23).

When Jesus speaks of opening and closing the door of heaven and of binding and loosing, He employs figurative language for the authority to forgive or to withhold forgiveness of sins. The Lord gives His church the power and authority to speak His Gospel to repentant sinners and to declare to unrepentant sinners that they are still under the wrath of God. The power of the Keys is the authority to speak Law and Gospel to individuals, with the assurance that such words are not empty but have the full authority of Christ. This power belongs to every believer; Christ entrusts it to the church.

Christ also instituted the Office of the Holy Ministry to publicly carry on the power of the Keys on behalf of His church. The first Christian congregation in Jerusalem had pastors who instructed new believers in the Word of God. These shepherds were the apostles whom Jesus had appointed. St. Paul affirms that among His gifts to the church Christ gave "some to be apostles, some to be prophets, some to be evangelists, and some to be pastors and teachers, to prepare God's people for works of service, so that the body of Christ may be built up" (Ephesians 4:11–12). The Office of the Holy Ministry is instituted by Christ: in God's plan of salvation, pastors are the Lord's servants in the public ministry of the Word and Sacraments.

ONE MINISTRY

God has entrusted the means of grace, Word and Sacraments, to all believers. As the apostle Peter affirms, they are God's royal priesthood. Christ's mandate to His church makes every Christian a witness for the Gospel. God builds and preserves His church through the ministry of the Word. Christ chose His apostles to begin the task of spreading the Word; they, in turn, have been followed by faithful ministers of the Word who have been called into the office of shepherd over God's flock.

Christ establishes only a single ministry for the building of His church: the ministry of the Word. "Ministry" may be used to refer to the rights, duties, and responsibilities that belong by Christ's ordering to the totality of the spiritual priesthood of believers. Every Christian—young or old, man, woman, or child—shares in this ministry as a believing, baptized child of God. By faith any Christian is a member of Christ's church and of the royal priesthood, possessing all the privileges and responsibilities of this royal station. Just as God's Old Covenant people, believers today are "a kingdom of priests and a holy nation" (Exodus 19:6).

Ministry also refers in a stricter sense to a specific office. For the sake of the church on earth, God instituted an office into which a qualified man is to be called by the believers gathered together at a specific place. The rights and responsibilities of the spiritual priesthood belong to all Christians, but they are not each to administer the means of grace publicly, as valid and efficacious as this would be. By divine institution the members of the royal priesthood are to call—that is, elect, choose, or appoint— qualified individuals to do this in their name and on their behalf.

The man called, therefore, does publicly by God's will what belongs to the ministry of the Word. A congregation does not surrender its rights and responsibilities when it calls a pastor, nor may any other power usurp them. The authority to call, elect, and ordain ministers is a gift given exclusively to the church.

God has established the pastoral office, and He fills it through the congregation's call. A God-given, wholesome, and blessed relationship exists between the royal priest- hood and the office of the public ministry. God is a God of order. By His divine ordering the office of the public ministry exists in and for the church. The fact that the work of the pastor is essentially the same as the ministry entrusted to all the "priests" proclaiming the Word is not intended by God to create an adversarial tension. On the contrary, these two lofty offices or stations, both institut- ed by God, must be understood as two poles of a sphere, around which the ministry of the Word turns, so that the Gospel may be smoothly and effectively preached in the world.

God Himself has willed and established the office of the public ministry. Christ, the Chief Shepherd of His church (1 Peter 5:4), called and appointed apostles for the founding of the church. He also provided for their suc- cessors in the preaching office (Acts 20:17, 28; 2 Timothy 2:2). The difference between the apostles and pastors is that the apostles entered their office through the direct call of Christ, their Lord; their successors, or undershep- herds, enter the preaching office through the call of the congregations they are to serve.

The apostle Peter recognizes his fellow elders or pastors who also tended the flock of God faithfully and humbly (1 Peter 5:1–4). Paul reminds the elders of the congregation at Ephesus that it is by the will of the Holy Spirit that they are to "be shepherds of the church of God, which He bought with His own blood" (Acts 20:28). Numerous other New Testament passages bear out the divine origin of the pastoral office (John 21:15–17; 1 Corinthians 3:5; 4:1; 12:28; Ephesians 4:11). The office of the Christian pastor, therefore, is grounded in God's express will and may be regarded as an extension of the apostles' office and therefore also of Christ's own ministry.

Christ promised He would be with His people, be they as few as two or three gathered together in His name (Matthew 18:20). He gives assurance that congregations will exist locally at given places, wherever His Word is heard and believed, until the end of time. No power in heaven or earth, not even the gates of hell, will prevail against the church He has instituted.

The office of pastor is necessary in the church; congregations are required by the Lord of the church to call qualified men into their service to minister publicly on their behalf. The church and the office of the public ministry, therefore, stand in a close relationship. When Christian congregations call pastors to serve them, they act at God's own express command. The pastoral office, or holy ministry, is a divine necessity tied to God's holy will for His church on earth.

DUTIES OR FUNCTIONS
OF THE PASTORAL OFFICE

The titles given to men who hold the office of the public ministry describe their functions or duties: elder, bishop or overseer, servant, teacher, and shepherd or pastor. The pastor is to preach and teach the Word publicly. He is to lead the congregation's formal, public worship services and publicly administer the Sacraments and the Office of the Keys. In general, he oversees the doctrine and life of the congregation in his care of souls. By accepting the congregation's call, the pastor exercises the functions of his office on behalf of and with accountability to the church that has called him.

Because pastors and the people they serve are members together of the priesthood of believers, there is no basic difference as to their persons. The only difference between them is one of office. Pastors are not priests by reason of their office. They are priests by faith and Baptism, like the members whom they serve. The latter, in turn, are not ministers or pastors by virtue of their priesthood, for they have not been rightly or regularly called into that office.

The power and validity of the Word and Sacraments are not dependent on the person or faith of the pastor, but on the authority of Christ and His Word. He alone prescribes the tasks of the Gospel ministry and makes this ministry effective. The pastor is Christ's servant and steward who strives to be found faithful by his Master (1 Corinthians 4:1; Acts 20:28).

At the same time, the pastor is the servant and steward of the congregation of royal priests, resolved in his heart for their sake "to present to you the word of God in its fullness," as St. Paul stated of himself (Colossians 1:25). The office he holds is a position of high trust. The pastor who has been duly called, who faithfully carries out his pastoral functions, and who earns the congregation's respect by his godly example will receive the honor and love of the people whom he serves.

While Scripture teaches and exhorts the highest respect for women, it is also true that God has excluded them from the pastoral office. This is God's ordering of things, and the church follows God's Word by calling baptized men to the office of the public ministry. St. Paul states in 1 Corinthians 14:34 that a woman is not to function as the presiding spokesperson (pastor/teacher) within a congregation. The apostle here is not judging adversely women's abilities, talents, and aptitudes. He simply grounds the prohibition against women holding the pastoral office in the natural order. By God's design and purpose, the office of the public ministry is to be conferred only on qualified men.

Auxiliary Offices

Other offices in the church derive from the one divinely instituted office and are therefore auxiliary to it. In the earliest history of the church, the apostles recognized the need to create additional offices to assist them in their multiple duties (Acts 6:1–15; Philippians 1:1). At various times and places men were designated deacons because of their service. Deaconesses are also spoken of in the early church. Phoebe, who carried Paul's letter to the congregation at Rome, distinguished herself in support of his ministry in other ways (Romans 16:1–2). The church has regularly responded with proper measures to meet and to support the ministry in its midst. The functions of these auxiliary offices, however, are instituted by God. They belong to the ministry of the Word.

Every position in the church, including the pastoral office, is one of service. The aim of all ministry is to convey new life in Jesus Christ to those who already have it, to those who stumble, and to those who have yet to hear the Gospel. God's servants seek the protection, comfort, and strength that come only from the Good Shepherd who first laid down His life for the sheep.

Excommunication

In dealing with a fellow congregation member who has sinned, the Christian church should not hastily declare him excluded from heaven. If we become aware that a brother or sister in the faith has committed a faith-destroying sin, we should in all kindness speak "the truth in love" (Ephesians 4:15). The goal is always to lead the person to repentance and faith. If our private efforts fail, we are to approach the erring brother or sister with the assistance of one or two other Christians. If this attempt also proves futile, we inform the whole congregation of the matter so that all may urge the sinner to repent. Only after such joint admonitions have failed is the offender to be excommunicated—considered outside the kingdom of God and Christ's church.

The declaration that an unrepentant person is no longer a member of the Christian church is the most solemn use of the authority to withhold forgiveness. Excommunication does not imply that because the whole congregation speaks, the door of heaven is closed more securely than when an individual Christian declares the wrath of God. Its unique feature is that an unrepentant sinner is excluded not only from heaven but also from the congregation. This action is recognized also by sister congregations as authoritative and valid. We must not forget, however, that God intends the severity of this action to have a beneficial result. God wants to bring people to an awareness of their sin so that they will turn to the Lord in true repentance (1 Corinthians 5:3–5).

Excommunication is a serious matter; the congregation exercises its authority and God-given rights after all other means of restoration have failed. It is not the act of an individual but of the congregation, though the pastor naturally is the spokesman of the church. Similarly, when the offender has repented and the excommunication can be revoked, the whole congregation declares him or her pardoned. Repentance and faith are always occasions for rejoicing!

The church believes that our ministry is Christ's ministry: to bring salvation to the world. With grateful hearts we pray, "Send us, Lord, into Your harvest fields."

·11·

Last Things

What happens when our life on earth is over? What will happen at the end of history? Though surrounded by anxiety and trouble, God's people confess that Jesus Christ is Lord. The Savior lives and orders all things according to His purpose. In quiet confidence, we trust that our life and death, our present and future, are secure in His hands. Our loving God works in everything, we believe, to keep us firm in faith and ready to meet Him in eternal glory.

DEATH

God did not create people to die. Sin brought this fate upon humanity (Genesis 2:17; Romans 5:12; 6:23). Ecclesiastes 12:7 describes the nature of death: "The dust returns to the ground it came from, and the spirit returns to God who gave it." At death, body and soul (or spirit) are separated. The body decays, while the soul of the believer goes to God. At His death Jesus, too, gave up His spirit (John 19:30; Luke 23:46).

IMMORTALITY OF THE SOUL

What happens to the soul after death? Some believe that death ends existence; without a soul, at death we dissolve into atoms and personal existence ceases.

Even many without faith in Jesus, however, believe that humans have some sort of existence after death. Some ancient philosophers affirmed the immortality of the human soul. Some people today worship their ancestors, a practice that presupposes belief in the continued existence of the soul. Matthew 10:28 and Luke 23:43 show clearly that the human soul does continue to exist after the body dies.

The Soul after Death and before Resurrection

While intuition may lead to the belief that the human soul continues to live after death, only God can reveal the nature of that existence. The Scriptures assure us that the souls of believers enter heavenly bliss immediately after the death of the body. The promise of Jesus to the repentant criminal offers glorious comfort to believers (Luke 23:43).

St. Paul also writes, "For to me, to live is Christ and to die is gain. If I am to go on living in the body, this will mean fruitful labor for me. Yet what shall I choose? I do not know! I am torn between the two: I desire to depart and be with Christ, which is better by far; but it is more necessary for you that I remain in the body" (Philippians 1:21–24). For the apostle death meant full life with Christ, being in Christ's presence, a far better state than earthly life. The New Testament often speaks of the death of Christians as a sleep (1 Corinthians 15:18; 1 Thessalonians 4:13; Acts 7:60). As forgiven sinners we need not look at death with anxiety and fear.

What happens to unbelievers after death? According to 1 Peter 3:19 their souls are kept "in prison," in a state identical with that of the fallen angels (2 Peter 2:4; Jude 6). Eternal punishment awaits the unbeliever, as the parable of the rich man and Lazarus teaches (Luke 16:19–31).

At death, then, the eternal fate of an individual is sealed. The verdict pronounced on the Last Day merely confirms the judgment passed on each person at death— eternal life or eternal punishment. The parable of the rich man and Lazarus shows that the state into which believers and unbelievers enter when they die is unchangeable. No opportunity for conversion exists after death.

The Last Times

The Scriptures refer to the time of the church as "the

last hour" (1 John 2:18); the "end of all things is near" (1 Peter 4:7). Though the apostles wrote these words centuries ago, "with the Lord ... a thousand years are like a day" (2 Peter 3:8). The great salvation of God on which our faith rests is finished. Nothing remains but the solemn conclusion to God's eternal plan. Christ has promised that He will come again in glory. We trust His Word. We believe and confess that the end of the world may come soon.

"When will these things happen?" the disciples asked their Lord. "What will be the sign that they are all about to be fulfilled?"

Jesus taught His disciples to wait for His return in hope and anticipation. Many signs will precede His Second Coming: wars and rumors of war, earthquakes and famines, persecution and days of distress (Mark 13:5–23). He warns His followers about false Christs and prophets. He calls us to be on guard, to watch, and to pray. By the Spirit's power, we live confidently, expecting our Lord to return at any moment.

In fact, many of the signs that our Lord described have come to pass. Natural disasters have occurred and are still occurring. Wars have often harassed the nations of the earth. The Gospel is being preached throughout the world in different ways. Spiritual woes, religious persecution, false teachers—all of these signs have taken place. The Last Day, it seems, may be close at hand.

Yet the ministry of the church goes on. The Lord calls and equips us to witness to His Gospel in our communities and around the world. We are like servants left in charge of the Master's house: we work faithfully while He is away, and we look forward to the day He returns. We know that Jesus will take us "home" with Him for eternity (Mark 13:32–37).

Many people believe Revelation 20 teaches that before the end comes we will experience a millennium; for a thousand years, they assert, Christ will reign on earth, suppressing the forces of evil. We must interpret this chapter in the light of other clear passages of Scripture. Suffering and persecution will remain until the end (Acts 14:22; Matthew 24 and 25; Mark 13; Luke 17 and 21). The kingdom of Christ is a spiritual kingdom, not an earthly one (John 18:36). The "thousand years" (Revelation 20:2) simply refers to a long period of time, the time from Christ's first coming until He comes again. Properly understood, the millennium represents the age of the church, as the Holy Spirit works to call sinners to faith and to equip God's people to proclaim the Gospel. The Lord God will carry out and complete the mission He has given to the church.

THE RESURRECTION OF THE BODY

When the Last Day comes, the bodies of all who have lived and died will become alive. God clearly reveals this truth in His Word.

- A time is coming when all who are in their graves will hear His voice and come out—those who have done good will rise to live, and those who have done evil will rise to be condemned.

- Christ has indeed been raised from the dead, the firstfruits of those who have fallen asleep. For since death came through a man, the resurrection of the dead comes also through a man. For as in Adam all die, so in Christ all will be made alive. But each in his own turn: Christ, the firstfruits; then, when He comes, those who belong to Him (1 Corinthians 15:20–23).

- We believe that Jesus died and rose again and so we believe that God will bring with Jesus those who have fallen asleep in Him. According to the Lord's own word, we tell you that we who are still alive, who are left till the coming of the Lord, will certainly not precede those who have fallen asleep. For the Lord Himself will come down from heaven, with a loud command, the voice of the archangel, and the trumpet call of God, and the dead in Christ will rise first (1 Thessalonians 4:14–16).

God also speaks of the resurrection of the body in the Old Testament (Exodus 3:6 [quoted by Jesus in Matthew 22:31–32]; Daniel 12:2; Job 19:25–27). The resurrected bodies of believers will be incorruptible, glorious, and strong, like the body of the risen Christ (Philippians 3:21).

Human reason cannot comprehend the miracle of the resurrection of the body. But we believe that because Christ is risen from the dead, we, too, will rise from the dead. Our soul and body will again be united, and all weaknesses and diseases from which our body suffers will have disappeared. With our glorified body we will enter eternal life in heaven with God. We look forward to the day of resurrection.

The Last Judgment

When Christ comes the second time, He will come as the Judge of the world (Acts 17:31). He will appear in glory (Matthew 25:31). All eyes will see Him (Revelation 1:7), and everyone will come before Him. Faith in Jesus the Savior, or lack of faith, will determine whether the Judge will acquit or condemn (John 3:18). The verdict will be righteous and just, as Christ will demonstrate by citing people's works. Those who performed good works on earth will have shown that they were Jesus' disciples, while those who performed evil works will have shown that they were not His disciples, for "without faith it is impossible to please God" (Hebrews 11:6).

Jesus' description of the last judgment does not mean that good works are the basis of our salvation. Rather, good works flow out of faith. By them we demonstrate that we are children of God. Because of the sacrifice of Jesus in our place and the faith we have received by the power of the Holy Spirit, we look confidently toward the Last Day. For all believers the sentence of the Judge will mean eternal happiness.

The End of the World

Heaven and earth will not last forever, but both will pass away (Luke 21:33; Hebrews 1:10–12; 1 Peter 4:7). The end will come on Judgment Day (2 Peter 3:7–10). God's Word does not reveal the precise nature of what will happen at the end of the world. Whatever happens, for Christians it will be a time of complete joy.

Eternal Damnation

In His description of the last judgment, Jesus said of the wicked: "They will go away to eternal punishment" (Matthew 25:46). These sad and terrifying words show that unbelievers will face an eternity of sorrow, pain, and separation from God. The Bible speaks both of the terrors of this condemnation and of its endless duration (Romans 2:9; Matthew 8:12; 18:8; 2 Thessalonians 1:9). The wicked will have to endure pain eternally and will not simply be annihilated.

We cannot say whether the condemned will be cast into a literal fire or if the Scriptures, in speaking of fire, use a figurative expression. The ultimate cause of a person's damnation is unbelief, the refusal to accept the forgiveness Christ has won even for the greatest sinner. We pray that the flame of faith, nourished by the Word and Sacraments, may never die within us.

Eternal Salvation

With grateful joy believers look forward to eternal salvation and the heavenly home. God gave His only Son so that those who believe in Him might not perish but have eternal life (John 3:16). This life consists in personally knowing God and Christ (John 17:3) and in fully experiencing His love. At the last judgment we shall behold our Savior and become like Him (1 John 3:2). All sin and weakness will then have ceased, and our body will be glorious and free from every imperfection (1 Corinthians 15:42–44). We do not receive eternal life because of our own efforts or achievements. It is a gift of God's love, prepared by Him and given to all who trust in Christ and receive forgiveness of sins.

Where is heaven? The Scriptures often speak of heaven in local, spatial terms, but they emphasize its joy. We will be in the presence of the Christ (1 Thessalonians 4:17; 1 John 3:2; Revelation 21:3). In heaven we will experience unending fellowship with God and the Lamb.

The promise of eternal life through Christ our Savior strengthens us in tribulation, draws our hearts away from worldliness, and makes us more eager to use the means of grace and to serve God and one another. Above all, it helps keep alive in us the triumphant faith that dwelt in St. Paul: "The Lord will rescue me from every evil attack and will bring me safely to His heavenly kingdom. To Him be glory for ever and ever. Amen" (2 Timothy 4:18).

The church in faith waits for the Lord Jesus to return and take us to heaven. Baptized in Christ, we now have eternal life through faith. Yet at the Last Day we will know the fullness of life and salvation. So we pray with one voice, "Come, Lord Jesus."

·12·

Life in Christ

The Christian church is a worshiping community with a unique faith. We believe in the triune God. We live in Christ. We grow through the preached and sacramental Word. We may not always be able to explain precisely what we believe or why we worship and pray the way we do, but we are certain that we belong to our Lord.

He is present with us. In worship we are engaged in something supremely important: hearing His Word in faith and receiving His gifts in Baptism and the Lord's Supper. This is the foundation of our lives. Worship and Word, the Bible, the Sacraments, all these belong together in the church. The living Christ is present in the Divine Service; He is with us, in our midst, to serve us.

The church's faith centers on God's actions for us. Our triune God plans our rescue. He initiates the saving relationship. He resolves our dilemma and enters our world to redeem us from sin, death, and the power of Satan. God acts, and we are forgiven, restored people. Our response is thanksgiving and praise through Jesus Christ.

Life in Christ is God's gift to us. We are buried and raised with Christ in Baptism. We share in His suffering and death and now live in His resurrection victory. What happened to Christ happens to us in Baptism. He is the Savior and Lord who claims us as His own and remakes us into His image.

CALLED TO SERVE

The God who calls us to faith and salvation through the Gospel also calls us to serve. Life in Christ is a life of devotion to both God and other human beings; we live in loving service in the midst of daily life. The opportunities for serving are endless and overwhelming. God calls us individually, not to try to do everything that needs to be done, but rather to serve Him first through our family, our church, and our community. In order to do something significant for our Lord and for others, we do not have to step out of these relationships and go somewhere else. Rather we are to turn to those people with whom we live and work and please God by serving them, even in ordinary ways. Extraordinary needs and opportunities and a new call from God may draw us out of one context and into another. But we live today in faith.

God's calling or vocation gives great meaning, value, and dignity to the roles and relationships of our life. It is not an accident or only a matter of human will that we are members of this family or this congregation, or that we live in a certain community or work at a particular job. God has placed us in these contexts. He has done it for good and important reasons. He provides us with opportunities to speak and act for Him and to help others in His behalf. What we do for people in these contexts is recognized and accepted by our Lord as done for Him.

THE SHAPE OF LIFE IN CHRIST

In Christ we are new people. Our life is not simply an ideal or an abstraction, but a concrete reality—we are, with the strength of the Holy Spirit, striving to live for Christ. In addition to the new person who is attuned to God and responsive to Him, there remains in every Christian the "old person," the old self. The old person serves self. The new person delights in God, loves His Word, and is constant in prayer. The new person in Christ acts this way and seeks to live as a disciple. However, though defeated by Christ, the old person is also active within us, trying to negate and counteract the influence of the new nature.

A Life Lived for God

As new creations in Christ we are centered in God. We live in God and rest on the promises of God. Another way to put it is to say that we live by faith, and this also involves living for God. The highest purpose of the life lived for Christ is to fulfill His expectations, to accomplish His goals. This is life centered in God.

A natural and inevitable part of the life lived for God is obedience. In our culture "obedience" often has negative connotations: it suggests galling conformity to resented demands or demeaning surrender to the will of another. But to the believer, obeying God is a positive experience. It is glad surrender to a will that is recognized as higher and better than our own. The obedience of the new person is given, not in response to God's demands and threats (His Law), but rather in response to His love and promises (His Gospel). It reflects the gratitude of a loving child. The new person, moved and overwhelmed by God's generosity, looks for ways to show high regard for God. We are, and daily want to live as, disciples of the Lord Jesus.

Worship

Worship is joyful fellowship with God and with His people. Our relationship with God is our highest priority; we want to live for God, and we want to worship. We look forward to each opportunity to hear from God and to receive His love in Word and Sacraments. We cherish the opportunity to speak to God in prayer, to open up to Him, to share burdens, needs, desires, and joys. We also treasure the fellowship of other worshiping Christians, welcoming the time together to encourage them in their faith and discipleship, and to be encouraged by them. A variety of factors may add to the attractiveness of worship— appropriate music, art, architecture, and drama, for example. Yet the great attraction is God Himself. To encounter God and interact with Him is the supreme privilege. The worshipful response of the new person is surprisingly broad in scope. It is by no means confined to the sanctuary and to personal devotions. Ultimately, all of life and work done in faith becomes an occasion for recognizing God and His gifts and for responding with thanksgiving and praise.

WITNESS

As believers whose hearts and minds are fixed on God, who value God above all else, we share God's love with other people. We offer others the comfort and hope that God provides. The impulse to witness, to communicate the Good News of Jesus Christ, is planted in us right along with saving faith. It flourishes and bears fruit in Christlike actions and Christ-centered conversation. Our Christian witness is not just any information about God, but specifically the message of forgiveness and eternal salvation through the life, death, and resurrection of Jesus. We call attention to God's goodness and grace, helping others to realize and appreciate the same in their own lives. Concern for people, for their well-being and happiness, is another impelling source of witness. The realization that all people desperately need to know and trust God moves us to speak the Gospel and act it out at every opportunity. Ultimately, our witness comes from God. The Holy Spirit provides us with both insights and words to convey effectively the saving message to others.

SACRIFICE

Faith in God and devotion to Him lead to acts of sacrifice. To sacrifice is to put God above everyone and everything else, even above self. We are able and willing to do this because we are aware of God's own sacrifice for us. In faith we respond to the atoning death of Jesus Christ, an enormous, generous sacrifice. We live sacrificially, joyfully, confidently, and without self-pity. We live in Christ, who is the center of our existence and who has saved us by His sacrifice.

A Life Lived for People

Our relationship with Christ has a profound effect on our relationship with others. When by faith we follow Christ and in gratitude want to serve Him, Christ directs much of our interest and energy outward to our fellow human beings. Christians owe God love and service, and we want to give these to Him. Yet God "accepts" very little for Himself. Instead, He channels the bulk of our response toward the needs of the neighbor. To live for God includes living for people, being aware of others and sensitive to their needs, and reaching out to others in the ways that God reaches out to us. Faith, when alive and authentic, becomes active in love. The love of the believer for others is a reaction to and, in fact, an extension of God's love for us.

Love in Christ is not simply a variation or intensification of ordinary human love. Rather, it has divine and eternal elements. It is a gift and work of God, a replica of God's own love as well as our response to His love.

If I speak in the tongues of men and of angels, but have not love, I am only a resounding gong or a clanging cymbal. If I have the gift of prophecy and can fathom all mysteries and all knowledge, and if I have a faith that can move mountains, but have not love, I am nothing. If I give all I possess to the poor and surrender my body to the flames, but have not love, I gain nothing.

Love is patient, love is kind. It does not envy, it does not boast, it is not proud. It is not rude, it is not self-seeking, it is not easily angered, and it keeps no record of wrongs. Love does not delight in evil but rejoices with the truth. It always protects, always trusts, always hopes, and always perseveres.

Love never fails. But where there are prophecies, they will cease; where there are tongues, they will be stilled; where there is knowledge, it will pass away. For we know in part and we prophesy in part, but when perfection comes, the imperfect disappears. When I was a child, I talked like a child, I thought like a child, I reasoned like a child. When I became a man, I put childish ways behind me. Now we see but a poor reflection as in a mirror; then we shall see face to face. Now I know in part; then I shall know fully, even as I am fully known.

And now these three remain: faith, hope and love. But the greatest of these is love. (1 Corinthians 13)

Love is sacrificial, willing to put the interests and needs of the other ahead of our own. In Christ, we care enough about the well-being of others to sacrifice resources, convenience, comfort, or, if necessary, even life itself (1 John 3:16). We live in Christ in His love.

The church lives by faith in Christ. We live *in* Christ and treasure Him *above all else.* Connected to Him through His Word and Sacraments, we live to serve the world around us.

Our life is a gift from Christ. Praise Father, Son, and Holy Spirit!

> Almighty God,
> Grant to Your Church Your Holy Spirit
> and the wisdom which comes down from heaven
>
> that Your Word may not be bound
> but have free course and be preached
> to the joy and edifying of Christ's holy people,
>
> that in steadfast faith we may serve You and in the confession of Your name may abide to the end;
> Through Jesus Christ, our Lord. Amen.